CEO Guide to Doing Business in Australia

By Ade Asefeso MCIPS MBA

Second Edition

ISBN-13: 978-1499584653

ISBN-10: 1499584652

Publisher: AA Global Sourcing Ltd
Website: http://www.aaglobalsourcing.com

Table of Contents

Disclaimer

This publication is designed to provide competent and reliable information regarding the subject matter covered. However, it is sold with the understanding that the author and publisher are not engaged in rendering professional advice. The authors and publishers specifically disclaim any liability that is incurred from the use or application of contents of this book.

If you purchased this book without a cover you should be aware that this book may have been stolen property and reported as "unsold and destroyed" to the publisher. In this case neither the author nor the publisher has received any payment for this "stripped book."

Dedication

This book is dedicated to the hundreds of thousands of incredible souls in the world who have weathered through the up and down of recent recession.

To my family and friends who seems to have been sent here to teach me something about who I am supposed to be. They have nurtured me, challenged me, and even opposed me.... But at every juncture has taught me!

This book is dedicated to my lovely boys, Thomas, Michael and Karl. Teaching them to manage their finance will give them the lives they deserve. They have taught me more about life, presence, and energy management than anything I have done in my life.

Chapter 1: Introduction

Are you a CEO, consultant, or entrepreneur interested in entering or expanding your business activity in Australian market?

Then this Book is for you!

The objective of this book CEO Guide To Doing Business In Australia is to provide you with basic knowledge about Australia; an overview of its economy, business culture, potential opportunities and an introduction to other relevant issues. Novice exporters in particular will find it a useful starting point.

Trade has always been an important part of the UK-Australia relationship. The UK and Australia have a close and long-standing personal, political and economic relationship, cooperate closely on international affairs, share common legal systems, language and societal structure, and have developed similar policy responses to those pressures.

The commercial environment in Australia is regarded as exceptionally friendly and attractive to business, with room for growth. Australian willingness to give new products and ideas a try recommends the country as a good market to test the international appeal of a product or service.

Highly developed media and advertising sectors mean that copy and promotional material require little adjustment. Geography is an important factor too. Australia's proximity to the Asia-Pacific market can offer a secure place to be based, with expansion into other regional markets. Urban areas are mainly confined to the east, south and south-west coastlines. This is where the major cities are located.

In Australia, many familiar products and service providers are at hand. The advantages for a British business person in Australia are its historical links, common language, similar business and legal practices and similar technical standards.

Perhaps the most striking variance is the different role of government and attitudes towards that role, in the conduct of day to day business. In Australia, the Federal and State Governments have traditionally been more overt players in the economy than their counterparts in other countries.

Australia has many varying climatic conditions. The northern part is tropical all year round, whilst in winter (June-July-August) frost and snowfall is experienced in the South-Eastern states of Victoria and New South Wales, as well as Tasmania.

Historical perspective

In 1768 the British Admiralty instructed Captain James Cook to begin a search for the 'Great South Island' first reached by Dutch sailors in the early 17th century. The crew of The Endeavour subsequently landed at Botany Bay in April 1770 and claimed the island for the British. The government decided that, following the loss of Britain's American colonies, Botany Bay should become the new destination for British convicts under sentence of transportation. On 26 January 1788 the First Fleet, sailing under the command of Captain Arthur Phillip, reached Australia (26 January is celebrated annually as Australia Day). A penal colony was also established in Van Diemen's Land (later renamed Tasmania). In total more than 168,000 convicts were transported. But free settlers were also attracted to Australia by its agricultural potential and, from the 1850s, the discovery of gold. Exploration and expansion followed and by the 1890s, calls for the colonies of New South Wales, Western Australia, Tasmania and Victoria to federate became increasingly strong. Australia became a nation on 1 January 1901.

Chapter 2: Strengths of Australian Market

There's never been a better time to do business with Australia.

Australia boasts an outstanding economic track record and offers UK businesses a dynamic and dependable market in times of economic uncertainty. Add to that a technology-hungry and sophisticated business and consumer base, very similar language, culture, history and business practices, and have outstanding opportunities for British business.

The Australian economy has been ranked as the world's most resilient economy for six out of the last eight years and is currently one the best performing economies in the OECD, so it's a great place to be doing business right now.

According to the World Bank's Doing Business Report 2011, Australia is the 10th easiest country to do business in (the same as 2010) and the second easiest in which to start a business. A new business can be established in Australia within two days.

Australia is the fifth largest economy in the Asia-Pacific region, and the 14th largest economy in the world, with an annual average GDP growth rate from 1998 to 2009 of 3.5%.

In 2010, Australian GDP real growth was 3.3%. The national unemployment rate was just 5.0 percent in

July 2011 and Australian consumer confidence is up to 105.3 in April 2011 compared to 69.5 one year ago*. Over the past decade, inflation has typically been 2–3% and the base interest rate 5–6%, 3.6 %(annual) and 4.75 %(unchanged) respectively was reported in Q2 2011.

Australia's proximity to the world's fastest growing region, the Asia Pacific, gives a distinct advantage to UK companies looking to springboard into this region, especially when more than 1 million Australians speak an Asian language fluently and more than 4 million Australians speak a second language.

Australia's growing orientation towards its Asian neighbours is reflected in its economic policy. It is a key member of the Asia Pacific Economic Cooperation forum (APEC) and it's in the process of establishing free trade agreements with China and the Association of Southeast Asian Nations (ASEAN).

Opportunities in Australia

The sectors listed below have been identified as major areas of opportunity for British businesses:
- Science and innovation
- Financial services
- Mining and minerals
- Oil and gas
- ICT
- Biotechnology
- Agribusiness

- Energy
- Environmental technologies
- Business and consumer services
- Education and training

The economic and trade relationship between Australia and the UK remains immensely important to both countries. Many UK firms see Australia as an excellent trading partner. Australia's continuing outstanding economic track record has raised its profile as a destination for many companies.

Chapter 3: Why Australia

Australia has a proud record of originality in advanced engineering. It is the country that gave birth to the ultrasound scanner, the black box flight recorder and the Bionic ear. Part of this success is due to cross-fertilisation between R&D institutions and the manufacturing sector.

They help to commercialise technologies in specialist fields such as advanced composite structures or automotive technologies. As a result, manufacturing currently attracts more than $3.9 billion annually in R&D, or 39 per cent of all business expenditure on R&D. Today, advanced manufacturing accounts for around half of Australia's A$104 billion annual manufacturing output and is one of the fastest growing export sectors.

Australia is known for its strengths in design, reliability, logistics infrastructure, skilled workforce, productive business culture, innovative systems, sophisticated IP protection and world class R&D capabilities.

Furthermore improved market conditions are ahead for the Engineering sector due to the escalation of recently commenced projects. With an economy transforming due to major infrastructure programs now starting to flow, big contracting and engineering firms are firing in tenders for a piece of the multi-billion dollar action. For small companies this is a chance to work with the big guys and strengthen the bottom line. Engineering construction levels are expected to be maintained by continuing strong demand for commodities from developing countries, in particular China and to a lesser extent India. This not only means that additional engineering construction will be needed to expand mining capabilities, but also that additional port and rail capacity will be required to export commodities. The proposed introduction of the Government's Emissions Trading Scheme will also create engineering opportunities as companies implement more energy efficient technology. These factors are expected to cause private engineering construction work to expand rapidly over the next 5 to 10 years.

Australia has a record as an innovator and developer of advanced materials, and has substantial infrastructure in this area. These materials can be used to develop new components for existing or entirely new consumer goods, for the construction and packaging industries, for the aerospace industry and for military applications. Advanced manufacturing has become a prime avenue for inward investment. In 2006, the value of Foreign Direct Investment in Australian manufacturing reached A$60 billion.

Some industry sectors have attracted particular attention among overseas high-technology companies. These include: Boeing and BAE Systems for specialist aerospace components; Ford, General Motors, and Toyota in the automotive sector; BASF and DuPont in the chemicals industry; and Siemens in energy and water treatment technology.

Competitive strengths and opportunities exist in areas such as synthetic resins, speciality chemicals, moulded plastics, pigments, coatings, packaging, advanced polymers.

Chapter 4: Advanced Engineering Opportunities in Australia

Bulk handling market

The bulk handing industry covers a wide range of companies usually involved in processing a variety of primary goods.

Australia has a heavy dependence on bulk solids handling operations. While these operations range across the broad spectrum of the bulk handling field, a major emphasis is on the storage, handling and transportation of coal, mineral ores and agricultural products, notably grain, in large tonnages.

Export earnings from minerals and agriculture are very substantial, with those from minerals approximating 50% and agriculture 30%.

Heavy Industry and other non-building construction

This sector plays a vital role in the Australian economy. It provides the foundation on which other economic activity takes place. It is important to recognise that the future economy is, literally, built on the products of the heavy engineering and infrastructure sector.

This industry is mainly engaged in the construction of engineering projects or infrastructure such as:

railways, dams, irrigation systems, harbour or river works, water or gas supply systems, oil refineries (except buildings), pipelines, and in the on-site assembly of boilers, furnaces or heavy electrical machinery from prefabricated components, or in the general repair of such structures, machinery or equipment.

The mining industry generates around 10% to 15% of industry activity and approximately one-quarter of the demand for private sector contractors. Engineering construction work on mining projects ranges from initial mine and dam construction, removal of overburden, design and installation of plant and equipment, transport systems and the construction of mineral processing facilities.

Funding comes mainly from the State governments which hold responsibility for the delivery of essential services and public infrastructure.

Automated equipment for manufacture

Australia's broad and diversified manufacturing industry is served by a large range of specialised automation and robotics system suppliers able to deliver innovative and efficient automation solutions for any processing, manufacturing, handling, assembly or packaging requirements.

Multi-disciplinary engineering teams, with expertise in software design and robotics applications, enable development of integrated advanced automation systems with proven manufacturing technologies and processes.

Engineering Services and R&D

The expertise of Australian firms in design for manufacture ensures that manufacturers and suppliers can develop world-class products with increasingly sophisticated technology. A number of global firms, including GM Holden, Schefenacher and Robert Bosch have established R&D facilities in Australia to serve their international networks.

Automotive

The Australian automotive industry encompasses a wide range of activities including vehicle production, component production, tooling and design and engineering. It is an important part of the Australian economy, employing over 64,000 people and accounting for almost 6 percent of manufacturing employment. Value added to the sector totals more than $5.6 billion, representing 5.6 percent of the manufacturing sector's industry value added and 0.6 percent of gross domestic product (GDP).

In its submission to the Review, Ford Australia noted that Australia is one of only 15 countries that can take a car from concept all the way to full production.

Aero Australia's

Aerospace industry employs more than 20,000 highly skilled people and offers world-class capabilities and innovative technologies at competitive prices. A recent KPMG study found Australia had the second lowest costs in aircraft parts manufacturing of 11 countries, and significantly lower than the US, UK, Japan and France. Australia's reputation for quality in high technology applications has drawn many of the world's leading aerospace companies including: Boeing, BAE Systems, EADS, Smiths, GKN, Northrop Grumman, Thales and Saab; a number of specialist SMEs and most major airlines

Heavy Electrical Equipment Manufacturing

This industry is mainly engaged in manufacturing electric motors, generators, electricity transmission or distribution equipment, switchgear, transformers or other electrical machinery, equipment, supplies or components. This class also includes units mainly engaged in manufacturing powder, paste or crystal soldering or welding flux.

Precision Engineering

The precision engineering and automation industry forms the backbone of the manufacturing sector, providing the machines, tools and equipment needed to produce all manufactured goods. The industry covers tooling, machine tools, cutting tools and precision components. The Australian precision engineering industry is a clean, high-technology industry with vertical and horizontal networks among professional subcontractors and suppliers. Through collaboration and networking between specialist firms and partnerships with research establishments, precision engineering companies create innovative and technically advanced solutions, and new technologies to meet emerging demands.

Tooling

Australian precision machine tool builders have developed globally competitive solutions for many specialised and niche production processes. Among these companies, a number are recognised as international industry leaders in their specific fields. The industry also comprises a broad, strong capability in special purpose machine design and construction and the integration and tooling of CNC machinery and other standard equipment to provide turnkey production systems.

Chapter 5: Shipping Industry Opportunities in Australia

Australia, as an island nation, is particularly dependent on the shipping industry for importing goods and exporting Australian-made products. Australia relies on sea transport for 99% of its exports. A substantial proportion of domestic freight also depends on coastal shipping.

The major ports within Australia operate under their respective Port Authorities and the closer economic integration of Australia with the rest of the world has seen greater trade flows develop over the past 20 years. These trade flows have been supported by an increase in the use of containers as the means of exporting and importing commodities and manufactured goods.

There is substantial growth predicted in both bulk and container ports into the foreseeable future. For container ports long term growth will grow at a compound rate of about twice GDP which means anywhere between 4-7% pa, which means TEU throughput will double in about 10 years. Substantive investment in expanded capacity is underway in Brisbane (additional container terminal and third stevedore), Sydney (Port Botany expansion of 4 or 5 berths) and Melbourne (channel deepening). All these projects amount in round terms to about $1 billion in each case. In Fremantle plans for outer harbour development and inner harbour deepening are well underway.

For bulk ports strong demand for resources particularly from China and India is driving some huge investments in bulk/resource ports in particular as it relates to iron ore, coal and LNG. By way of example Port Hedland is undergoing a $2.5 billion expansion and increases in capacity of similar magnitudes are occurring at Dampier, Dampier, Gladstone, and Newcastle.

Currently the Federal Government alone is funding a $36 million rail and road investment program some of which is being applied to support access to ports and in increasing the efficiency of supply chains.

Pressure on infrastructure, and demand for example for rail rolling stock nationally remains intense, and in the ports sector for skilled people and consultancy services in the ports has not diminished over the course of the so-called GFC. (Interestingly the volume of resources being exported has not diminished at all although the value/price has been affected).

Furthermore Australia is now enjoying increasing volumes of export grains after some years of drought affected output.

The government owned ports are corporatized and accordingly subject to commercial disciplines. While subject in varying degrees to guidelines/policies (e.g. in relation to borrowings) of their respective central agencies they, in the main determine the providers and contractors for their services. In short, there is a lot going on, there is robust demand for engineering/coastal engineering/hydrographical and other related services, and the market is pretty open and port corporations directly purchase those services. There is a view that the market is ripe for better applications of IT to freight management.

There are Australian suppliers in specialist areas locally and overseas and likewise the corollary applies. In some areas such as dredging for example the tendency is to rely on overseas suppliers. There are home grown specialists in under keel clearance systems that are selling strongly in Europe.

For a full list of port corporations and data on the commodities that they handle this information go to the Ports Australia at www.portsaustralia.com.au. Ports Australia is the peak body representing the interests of ports and marine authorities in Australia. It has been in existence in one form or another since around 1910 and was incorporated under the New South Wales Associations Incorporation Act (1984) in 1989.

Port Authorities in Australia are owned by government although they do not as a rule own and operate (with some notable exceptions including common user facilities) stevedoring and other handling operations but are responsible for the strategic planning of their precincts and (increasingly) of their supply chains.

Privatised ports include Flinders Ports (SA) and the Port of Portland in Victoria. Brisbane Port

Corporation and Abbot Point in Queensland are in the process of being privatised.

There are a number of working groups within Ports Australia:

- Port Operations and Technology Group (which includes OH&S and Hydrographic/Marine Surveyors sub groups
- Accounting & Finance Group (which includes an IT sub groups)
- Engineers Group
- IR/HR Group
- Environment Group (which includes as Sustainable sub group)
- Port Security Group

All Groups have a wide representation from all states. These Groups exchange information and discuss issues that need to be investigated by the Association and its members and, in many cases; small specialist adhoc working groups are formed to develop a common view or approach. Ports Australia also runs seminars, conferences and working groups on a range of specific issues from time to time.

National Competition policy is assisting in developing a more competitive and efficient maritime sector through legislation review, competitive neutrality and structural reforms. Some States are also introducing third party access regimes covering shipping berth channels and port infrastructure. Further information regarding this issue, as well as other relevant documents can be found on the National Competitive Council website: www.ncc.gov.au

Chapter 6: Biotechnology Industry Opportunities in Australia

Australia is the leading location of Biotechnology in the Asia Pacific region. Australia has a thriving biotechnology sector including around 450 core biotech companies amongst an industry total of 1200 enterprises and a world class scientific, medical and agricultural research base.

Australia is ranked the 6th largest biotechnology industry in the world behind the US, UK, Canada, Germany and France. With beneficial exchange rates, a booming economy and proximity to the emerging markets of the Asia Pacific region, there has never been a better time to do business in Australia.

Companies looking to market services in drug discovery, development, clinical trials, contract manufacturing, Australia is the market to explore. Also for Biotechnology and pharmaceutical companies looking to partner with world-leading research institutions, license in projects at pre-clinical or phase 2 stages or license out technology particularly in the oncology and infectious disease space.

CSL, based in Melbourne, is Australia's largest biotechnology player and currently the 4th largest biotech company in the world based on sales and has a market cap around $20 billion.

CSL's key areas of expertise include blood plasma products, vaccines, antibodies and recombinant biotechnology. Major recent activity in the Australian biotech market has included US company Cephalon's $320 million takeover of Arana Therapeutics, Danish company Leo Pharma acquiring Peplin for $307 million, Acrux's $600 million licensing deal with Eli Lilly for its underarm testosterone treatment Axiron and Mesoblast's up to $2 billion deal with Cephalon for its stem cell therapies.

A recent industry survey showed that Australian biotechnology companies had 70 clinical trials underway, with over half of these in either phase 2 or phase 3. Australia's federal and state governments have targeted biotechnology as one of the innovative industries that will be key to economic growth. As such the industry has been historically built on publically funded R&D including universities, medical institutes and organisations such as CSIRO and compared with competing nations Australia produces a larger proportion of life science graduates.

There is still strong government support for biotechnology research, although as the sector matures governments are increasingly looking to fund projects particularly geared to commercialisation.

Victoria

Victoria, and its state capital Melbourne, is the largest centre for biotechnology in Australia. Comprising more of 140 companies, 13 major medical research institutes, eleven teaching hospitals and 9 universities,

Melbourne joins London and Boston as the only three cities in the world with two universities in the global top 20 biomedical rankings.

As part of initiatives to encourage the growth of the biotechnology industry Victoria has developed a number of Biotechnology Precincts with shared infrastructure between Universities Research Hospitals and private companies to encourage sharing of facilities and expertise. These include:

The Bio21 Cluster

The Bio21 Cluster links 22 research organisations to support shared infrastructure and expertise in biotechnology. The project has established the Bio21 Institute at the University of Melbourne and six collaborative infrastructure projects providing access to platform technologies such as high-throughput screening, informatics and protein crystallisation. It is also home to the Victorian Life Sciences Computation initiative.

Parkville Precinct

The Parkville Precinct is the major precinct in Australia for medical and bioscientific research, education, clinical practice, production of pharmaceuticals and biotechology products. Members include Melbourne Health, University of Melbourne, Walter and Eliza Hall Institute of Medical Research, Howard Florey Neurosciences Institute and the Ludwig Institute for Cancer Research.

Monash Health Research Precinct

Based around Monash University this precinct links the university and the Southern Healthcare network with major research organisation and infrastructure including CSIRO, the Australian Synchrotron and the Australian Stem Cell Centre.
New South Wales

Sydney is the traditional centre for pharmaceutical manufacture in Australia and a major proportion of global pharma companies and local generics companies are based here. These include Pfizer, Merck and AstraZeneca.

New South Wales also hosts 120 biotechnology companies, is a major centre for clinical trials Hearing, Wound Management Innovation, Beef Genetic Technologies and Invasive Animals.

Government Support

The Australian Federal Government joins the state governments in providing incentives and programmes designed to assist the development of the biotechnology industry. Some of these are available to both local and international companies.

The R&D Tax Credit is the Australian Government's principal initiative to encourage research and development (R&D), and includes expanded access to foreign companies who undertake R&D in Australia and to companies that hold their intellectual property offshore.

The R&D Tax Credit provides eligible companies with a tax offset for expenditure on eligible R&D activities. The two components of the program are: A 45 per cent refundable tax offset (equivalent to a 150 per cent deduction) for eligible R&D entities with a turnover of less than $20 million per annum;

A non-refundable 40 per cent tax offset (equivalent to 133 per cent deduction) for all other eligible R&D entities. Unused offset amounts can be carried forward for use in future income years.

Key Methods of Doing Business

As a general rule Australian Biotechnology companies, along with the major research institutes will actively look to partner with overseas companies.

The markets of the US and Europe are the key end target for Australian companies and they will particularly look for service providers with expertise in these markets to assist in the development of products.

Ability and knowledge of ways to access funding, for example from the European Framework 7 programme can be a big incentive for Australian companies looking to outsource or collaborate on R&D programmes. Business culture is commonly face-to-face in Australia so meeting potential clients more than once is a must. Targeting meetings at international events such as BIO or BioPartnering Europe, followed up by visits to Australia is a useful way to generate a relationship.

Chapter 7: Creative Industry Opportunities in Australia

Australia is a sophisticated, literate, multicultural market, with extensive traditional ties to the UK and strong links into Asia and is well positioned to offer an exciting range of opportunities to British exporters in the Creative Industries.

The main thrust of the export development focus for the UK creative industries to Australia continues to be in design, incorporating product design (particularly residential and commercial furniture, lighting, packaging and home accessories), industrial and graphic design, film, television (specifically digital multi-media) and music. British companies are well positioned to deliver expertise in the creative industries.

British expertise has a good reputation in Australia and the ever increasing positive perception of Creative Industries in corporate Australia provides lucrative opportunities for UK creative firms.

A positive perception of the Creative Industries is expanding in corporate Australia as businesses realise its value. This is evident in activity such as more businesses joining in annual design competitions, an increase in design related trade exhibitions and festivals, and the establishment of a "Creative Industries" faculty at Queensland University of Technology.

Design

For British design companies the market in Australia is looking increasingly attractive. British design is seen as a world leader in Australia, especially in the area of new media, and the Australian market is becoming a very real proposition for forward-looking British companies with global ambitions.

Part of the reason so many British companies made the move to expand into Australia is the close proximity of the Asian markets. Companies that have serious global aspirations must look towards these areas, and many are coming to realise that Australia is the key.

There is a growing appreciation by the Australian Federal and State Governments of the importance of design in providing competitive advantage, innovation and economic success.

Film and Television

Australians are avid cinema-goers – the fourth highest per capita in the world. The domestic industry produces an average of 20 feature films per year, and the five free-to-air television networks show their quota of Australian drama, documentary and children's programming. The overall production industry is worth almost $A 2.082 billion. The overwhelming trend is towards an international industry.

Australia has seen a significant rise in the number of co-productions and foreign films choosing to shoot in Australia. This has increased the transfer of knowledge, skill levels and talent base of crews and actors, as well as contributing to the technical equipment base of the Australian post-production sector. At the same time, the mainly government-funded domestic industry, through state and federal film bodies and training institutions, has produced international stars and behind-the-camera talent who are in demand worldwide.

Film: The Australian Government has official co-production arrangements with the United Kingdom. This allows UK companies filming in Australia to take advantage of tax concessions.

The objective of film co-production treaties and less-than-treaty arrangements is to foster cultural development and cultural exchange by facilitating international film co-productions.

Film co-productions also: open up new markets for Australian films; enable creative interchange; strengthen existing diplomatic ties between countries; and Increase the output of high quality productions through the sharing of equity investment.

Television: A subscription television station dedicated to British programs has existed for 7 years in Australia.

Mobile Content

Australia has four mobile carriers, Telstra Optus, Vodafone, and Hutchison (Three) in order of market share. All are keen to offer premium services to differentiate them from their competitors. This offers opportunities for suppliers of high quality content.

Chapter 8: Interactive Media Opportunities in Australia

Interactive Media is a high growth industry in Australia with most companies based in Sydney, Melbourne and Brisbane. The Australian Interactive Media Industry Association (AIMIA), founded in 1992, assists companies working in this sector. AIMIA is the peak national industry body representing the Interactive Media and Digital Content sectors in Australia.

AIMIA are devoted to the commercial development of the industry as a whole and to the commercial development of the distinct AIMIA members and AIMIA member groups that comprise the Interactive Media and Digital Sectors.

Digital multi-media

As per data from ITU website over 15 million Australians use the internet, whilst broadband has only 5.14 million subscribers. However, on April 7, 2009 the Government announced it would soon begin the process to establish the National Broadband Network. This will surely increase the amount of broadband consumers as well as the level on usage per capita. There is much opportunity in the transference of print and broadcast media to digital media.

Music

Recorded music retailing Industry sales for 2009-10 falls by 2.5% to $1.12 billion. Electronic Component Manufacturing in Australia also experience reductions in revenue to $2.441billion. There are approximately 430 professional sound recording studios in Australia.

Performing Arts

Mid-scale productions from the UK have had successful tours to Australia in recent times. The Sydney Theatre Company has a British influence in several of its subscription season productions this year.

Computer/video Games

Most of Australia's computer games development industry is based in Victoria and Queensland. Over 800 people are employed in the industry in Melbourne. Melbourne has a 20-year history in computer game development, largely due to Beam Software, purchased in 1999 by France's Infrogrames, now Atari.

The primary activities of this industry are:
- Game software development
- Game software publishing
- Games software retailing
- Games software manufacture
- Console development
- Console manufacture

- Console retail
- Accessories development
- Accessories retail
- Online game subscription revenue

The major products and services in this industry are:
- Software Retail
- Hardware Retail
- Software Publishing
- Online Subscriptions
- Software Development
- Other Development
- Manufacturing

Annual Australian combined computer software and hardware sales are estimated to be around A$825 million. The Games Developers Association of Australia (GDAA), with support from the Victorian and Queensland State Governments, has recently completed a national survey of the Australian games industry.

The primary activities of this industry are:

PCs, desktop units, notebooks and laptops retailing Peripherals retailing (scanners, printers, keyboards, CDROM and DVD-ROM drives) Packaged computer software retailing (except games)

The major products and services in this industry are:

Home computer equipment (including pre-packaged software), Computer software and Blank computer media

Publishing Industry

This industry is a broad range of newspaper, books and stationary including fiction and non-fiction books, educational books, newspapers, comics, magazines and other printed material. The total industry revenue during 2008/09 was $7.8billion.

Books accounted for 33% of all sales where as newspapers and magazines were 21% and 16% respectively. The level of industry concentration is very low, with major competitors accounting for 40% of the total market share in 2009/10. As a result, in 2009-10 the majority of establishments for this industry will be located in NSW (35%), Victoria (22%) and Queensland (20%).

Chapter 9: Education and Training Opportunities in Australia

Australia's education system has a worldwide reputation for excellence in all areas of learning and diversity of opportunity. Australia is a sophisticated, literate, multicultural market, with extensive traditional ties to the UK and strong links into Asia and is well positioned to offer an exciting range of opportunities to British exporters in the Education sector.

British expertise has a good reputation in Australia and increasing demand for quality education and training, along with increased Government spending in this sector provides significant opportunities.

There are opportunities for British companies to capitalise on new initiatives and programs across the Australian education sector.

The Australian education was modelled initially on the British system. Primary and secondary school education is traditionally followed by vocational or University education.

Despite the common starting point the immense geographical size of Australia and the states' and territories' isolation from each other has led to each state developing some peculiarities and differences in the delivery of education and training.

Links between Australian and UK educational institutions and policy makers are strong and renewed regularly by exchanges of ideas and people. The UK has a strong reputation in this sector built on these continued links.

Australia provides an excellent opportunity for UK companies to internationalise. The Australian people think in a similar way to us and respond to similar incentives. There is a ready market for UK products and services. Doing business is relatively straightforward and reflects much of the practice found in UK. Solid intellectual property laws, and familiar business regulations reduces the risks of exporting goods and services to Australia.

There are opportunities for British companies to capitalise on new strategies across Australia to align education delivery with national standards and curriculum. This strategy is currently filtering from tertiary level downwards, with a national curriculum for schools being implemented. Although the education sector is predominantly public funded and domestically oriented, private providers and export markets have drive recent growth.

Vocational education for example can be offered by private companies. British companies can register and deliver training in Australia.

Also sought in Australia are Special Needs education, multi-equal opportunities and new teaching methods which British suppliers can provide.

Other areas where Australia could absorb proven UK educational products include "Curriculum Online" type initiatives. Experienced UK companies offering these types of e-products to a large population in the UK will have an advantage in Australia.

Early Childhood

Indigenous Early Childhood National Partnership Agreement – $292.6 million over 5 years to establish a minimum of 35 Children & Family Centres across Australia by 2014.

Early Years Learning Framework – Describes the principles, practice and outcomes essential to support and enhance young children's learning from birth to five years.

Schooling

Digital Education Revolution - The $16.2billion Digital Education Revolution will enhance access to new technology in schools across Australia.

Trade Training Centres Program – The $2.5 billion Trade Training Centres in Schools Program is building new infrastructure to develop vital skills and talents.

Building the Education Revolution – The $16.2 billion BER program aims to modernise schools through the delivery of necessary infrastructure, and by doing so, support local jobs and stimulate investment.

Literacy and Numeracy in Schools – Government is providing significant additional funding through collaborative new National Partnerships with states and territories to improve teacher quality ($550 million), boost literacy and numeracy ($540 million) and raise achievement in disadvantaged school communities ($1.5 billion).

Higher Education

Education Investment Fund – The Education Investment Fund will deliver new capital expenditure, and renewal and refurbishment to Australia's higher education and vocational education and training institutions. The Government has already invested $8.7 billion in the fund.

Australia Government will provide an additional $5.4 billion to support higher education and research over the next 4 years in a comprehensive response to the Bradley Review, Transforming Australia's Higher Education System.

Skills & Training

Productivity Places Program (PPP) is to provide targeted training to support the development of skills in Australia to meet existing and future industry demands

The Teaching and Learning Capital Fund (TLCF) (VET) – will provide $500 million which will be distributed through initiatives focused on modernising and improving the quality of teaching and learning across the vocational education and training sector.

Vocational Education Broadband Network (VEN) – The $80 million funded program will improve national infrastructure and support the use of interactive e-learning materials, virtual classrooms and real time access to content collections for TAFEs and learners.

Chapter 10: Rail Opportunities in Australia

The Australian rail market is attractive and, growing and is already providing activity to UK companies as well as to International competitors. Current exchange rates favour exporters from Australia, certainly in the short term, but in order to succeed, UK companies need to demonstrate they are competitive, and that they can service their target market and customer. Preparation, market awareness and intelligence are all vital to success.

According to a number of informed commentators, there is a need to improve infrastructure in Australia in general, not just in the Rail Sector. There is a belief that investment has been insufficient over the past twenty years to maintain pace with growth and certainly has been insufficient to facilitate growth in future.

Sustainable transport is required to ensure the country can remain economically competitive. Forward planning strategies advocate the use of extended public, integrated transport, and improved port connectivity for freight. Such strategies will benefit the Rail Sector. Most existing infrastructure is owned by State Governments, but maintenance is generally out-sourced to the private sector and operations are franchised generally on a long term basis.

Existing passenger systems in the country are heavily subsidised. They are working at, or near capacity, so extensions and / or systems are planned. The focus will be on delivering better services to passengers and adding freight capacity. The existing system of rail regulation, which is currently managed at state level, has hindered inter-state rail traffic, but this may change in the medium-term with the move to a single nationwide regulator.

UK companies seeking to enter the Rail market in Australia are likely to encounter both the Public and Private sectors. State Governments are very important in railways due to Track ownership, franchising system and regulatory powers.

They are also keen to maintain economic activity and develop the skills base within their State where possible, and UK companies should be aware of this sensitivity.

The Australian rail market is diverse, and can be segmented into heavy haul, (mainline) freight, and passenger, each of which is expanding. Recent high profile projects announced include the creation of a Metro in Melbourne, the Gold Coast Rapid Transit, Waratah Coalfield (now re-named China First), the Galilee Basin Coal Field and Railway, and the Oakajee Port and rail development on the West Coast. There is a proposal to privatise part of Queensland Rail (QR); the country's only remaining vertically integrated railway.

Certainly, Australia has a sizeable indigenous railway industry. However, there are skills, products and service gaps in the market, and a desire for advanced but proven technology. Engineering and signalling skills shortages are frequently cited, but opportunities for UK companies extend into all areas of activity.

The rail industry in Australia is investing in both the freight and passenger sectors within a context of investment in infrastructure in general. Estimates put planned projects and capital investment in railways at around Au$ 36bn, (£22bn) in a country which has not only ridden out the global financial crisis (GFC) rather well, but whose resource industries and major cities are planning significant expansion.

(Note that in Australia, the economic crisis is usually referred to as the "GFC", being the global financial crisis.).The resource industries based around the minerals and the hydrocarbon sectors are both robust. The major markets for minerals, in particular China, appear to be recovering and the Australian hydrocarbon sector, particularly gas, is ramping up.

Indeed, a number of informed commentators in Australia have been advocating investment in infrastructure to support economic growth for some time, pointing out that it is much needed, given the modest investment over a prolonged period - as much as 20 years, according to some.

The railway sector is progressive in its approach. Its preference is for advanced technology, but technology that is proven rather than emergent. Balanced consideration is given to the environment in transport planning, and a positive approach to sustainability is prominent in public transport policy.

Public transport is widely used, perhaps as a result of heavily subsidised fares, and most systems are working at, or near, capacity in the major cities. Therefore, significant plans for expansion of all types of public transport (heavy and light rail, as well as tram and bus services) are in hand within Transport Blueprints at State Government level. These are supported, in some cases, by a national infrastructure plan and budget. Add the activity from the resource sector and you have a thriving railway sector.

One consequence of all of this is that a diverse array of skills is in demand across a wide range of disciplines, including both blue and white collar disciplines.

Sustainability and Climate Change

The debate over climate change is taking place in Australia, as in other parts of the world. One context for the transportation sector is carbon pricing, where rail does appear to offer advantages over road and air transport in view of its comparably lower carbon emissions. Yet other issues also need to be taken into account in Australia, with its unique population distribution, densities and the huge distances travelled. For example, the roads sector has traditionally been active even for long distance freight. The reason for this is that rail connections to ports are under-developed and, in the busy city areas, enhancing freight rail corridors is only now getting underway. It could be a major and expensive task.

An example is the Melbourne to Sydney corridor. High speed rail has long been mooted for what is one of the world's busiest air corridors. Though widely discussed, many question whether the cost of building a high speed link would be economically viable due the distance and the finite size of the passenger market.

Australia has a robust indigenous industry in the rail sector, but there are skills shortages which will continue to present opportunities to UK companies and international competition in what is an expanding market. Market research is vital before entering any new market and Australia, like all markets, has its own unique character.

Specifications are generally based around Australian standards, but international quality standards are recognised, and are reasonably well accepted. There is a desire to increase efficiency, and a desire for advanced, proven technology.

Indeed, the significant growth in UK passenger and freight rail on track that was achieved without a corresponding increase in network size would be an attractive proposition in Australia where many networks are approaching capacity.

One useful strategy when considering market entry is to approach the market via existing contacts or customers. Australian contractors have been active overseas, and UK as well as Australian and international consultancies are active in the market. Australia is a transparent market and encourages international participation, yet addressing local content, is a key aspect for success.

Tender information is released by diverse means, but use of electronic notices is increasing. Generally, those companies that have a presence in some form within Australia are more likely to succeed than those seeking to service the market from offshore. As State Governments seek to ensure best value for money and protect employment within their own territory, only businesses deemed to be within the state boundary may represent a truly "local" offer, hence, a local partner or presence can be helpful. Local content can be addressed in a variety of ways; it doesn't just imply creating a local business presence. There is usually an informal network in the market, and meeting clients face-to-face is always vital.

Local Presence can be addressed in a number of ways Agents, distributors or partners can fulfil the role of local partner, and AA Global Sourcing Ltd http://www.aaglobalsourcing.com can provide tailored information and assistance to help companies to find them.

Remember UK companies may find the Australian market not unlike the UK, where value across the life cycle is increasingly the standard measured. Other aims of the market include reducing energy costs and improving service to customers, in both passenger and freight. Another similarity with the UK is the need to enhance capacity on existing infrastructure, especially within crowded urban areas where building new track may not be an option. Although the

Australian market may be similar to UK market, it is important to recognizes, however, that it is different and unique and to treat it as such.

The relative exchange rates are also favourable to UK companies, at the time of writing, with a strong dollar and a relatively weak pound. This enables UK companies to demonstrate even better value in the market. With no language barriers, commonly derived laws and railway standards, (although locally adapted), the Australian market may well be a very attractive one to UK companies.

Market Entry and Growth

Whilst there are opportunities, there is also competition, and some barriers to trade. There is, in many respects, a thriving and progressive local rail industry, as well as wider international competition. Australia sees itself firmly in the Asia Pacific sphere of influence, with an upward trend in trade and outlook. Distance is one consideration, even if language is not. Specification and standards vary from place to place, and choice of location and a local presence are also essential elements of the business mix.

Immigration and work permits require thought. Law is very close to English law but, as ever, professional advice is recommended.

Chapter 11: Agricultural Opportunities in Australia

Australia is globally recognised as a one of the world's most efficient producers of quality agricultural products.

Australia's vast landscape and mix of climate zones has produced a very advantageous and lucrative position. The producers within Australia are able to provide a myriad of products, much more than the domestic market can currently consume, thus they turn to the profitable export markets to fill the gap. With government spending large amounts on infrastructure it is becoming logistically easier to export and import products and produce.

Looking forward, agricultural revenue is anticipated to generate an average growth rate of 4.5% per annum and global demand conditions are expected to improve.

There are opportunities across the spectrum of agriculture, horticulture and aquaculture for UK companies with technically innovative products bringing productivity and efficiency gains or novel solutions. However, these sectors, like most in Australia, are very cost sensitive.

Wheat

The total area sown to wheat for grain in 2008/09 was 14.15 million hectares (mil ha).

The three main growing states were Western Australia, New South Wales and South Australia. The estimated total area sown in 2009/10 is 13,788-mil ha. The three main growing states estimated growing states will remain the same.

Production of wheat for grain in 2008/09 rose from the previous 5-year average to 20.938-mil t. The top 3 producers were Western Australia, New South Wales and South Australia. It is estimated that in 2009/2010 production will increase to 21.656 mil t.

Barley

The total area sown to barley for grain in 2008/09 rose from the previous 5-year average to 4.790-mil ha. The main growing states were Western Australia, South Australia and Victoria. The estimated sowing area in 2009/10 is 4.479-mil ha, with Western Australia Sowing, South Australia and New South Wales sowing the majority.

Production of barley for grain in 2008/09 fell to 7.669 million tonnes from the previous 5-year average. Major producing states were Western Australia, South Australia and New South Wales. The estimated production in 2009/10 is 8.048 million tonnes with Western Australia South Australia, Victoria producing the most.

Grain sorghum

The total area sown to sorghum for grain in 2008/09 reduced slightly to 752,000 ha from the previous 5 year average.

Queensland and New South Wales are the most prominent growers. The estimated sowing area in 2009/10 is 429,000 hectares.

Production of sorghum for grain in 2008/09 rose from the previous 5-year average to 2.671mil ha. Production again concentrated in Queensland and New South Wales.

Oats

The total area sown to oats for grain in 2008/09 fell to 856,000 from the previous 5-year average. The three main growing states were Western Australia, New South Wales and Victoria. The total estimated sowing area in 2009/10 is 909,000 ha.

Production of oats for grain in 2008/9 fell from the previous 5-year average to a total of 1.205-mil t. The estimate for production in 2009/10 is 1.244 mil t.

Other crops

In 2008/09 the total area sown to Canola was 1.670 mil ha with an estimated 1.395 mil ha to be allocated in 2009/10. The area planted to Sugar Cane for crushing was 367,000 ha, and the area planted to cotton was 164,000 ha.

The area sown to Lupins for grain was 578,000 ha, and the area sown to Rice was 8,000 ha.

In 2008/09, Canola production was 1.861-mil t, Lupins for grain production was 716,000 t, and Rice production was 63,000 t. The production of Sugar Cane cut for crushing was 30.284-mil t and the production of Cotton Lint was 176,616 t.

Chapter 12: Livestock and Agricultural Machinery Opportunities in Australia

Milk cattle

Preliminary estimates indicate the number of milk cattle in Australia was 1.65 million head during 2008/09. Victoria continued to dominate the dairy industry with 1.04 million head. Over 40,000 people are directly employed on dairy farms throughout Australia. There are opportunities for veterinary, milking and husbandry equipment.

Meat cattle

Preliminary estimates for 2009 indicate the number of meat cattle in Australia was 27.32 million head. The dominant states in the industry were Queensland and New South Wales. Consumption of beef within Australia alone is expected to rise 10% within the next 5 years.

Sheep and lambs

Preliminary estimates at the end of 2009 indicated the number of sheep and lambs in Australia was 71.56 million head. The dominant states in the industry were New South Wales, Western Australia with and Victoria.

Pigs

Preliminary estimates at the end of 2007 indicated the number of pigs in Australia was 2.23 million head. The dominant states in the industry were New South Wales and Queensland.

Agricultural Machinery

The agricultural machinery industry produces a wide variety of farm-related products. Output may be categorised into six broad types of product that are based on the end-use. These are:
  a. Tillage implements;
  b. Seeding and fertilising machinery;
  c. Harvesting and haymaking machinery;
  d. Tractors;
  e. Lawn Mowers; and
  f. Other agricultural machinery (such as grinder mixers, wool presses and windmills).

By far the largest segment of UK agricultural equipment sales to Australia is tractors. Australia is the 9th largest market for UK tractors, valued at around £23m in 2005, and the 18th largest market for agricultural machinery, valued around £4m in 2005.

It is an intensely competitive sector with 32 brands of tractor in the market. (This is indicative of the agriculture sector generally.) Other prominent segments (by export value) for UK suppliers are portable sprayers, soil cultivation machinery, weeders, hoes, grass trimmers and parts/replacement wear parts.

Moderate growth is forecast for the industry in 2011-12, driven by improving economic conditions and forecast stronger agricultural production volumes. Assuming a return to average seasonal conditions, farm income is expected to increase as production rises and feed costs remain relatively low, encouraging farmers to invest in capital equipment.

Chapter 13: Fisheries and Aquaculture Opportunities in Australia

Fisheries

The gross value of production of Australia's fisheries and aquaculture products was $2.18billion in 2008/09. The value of edible and non-edible fisheries product was $2.182 billion; $1.194 billion being exported. Australia's main seafood export earners include rock lobsters, prawns, tuna and abalone.

Australia's fisheries span oceanic, coastal, estuarine and freshwater regions and involve commercial, indigenous and recreational aspects. Australia's exclusive economic zone (EEZ) is the third largest in the world, covering about 10.3 million square kilometres.

The commercial sector of the fishing industry is Australia's fourth most valuable food-based primary industry - after beef, wheat and dairy.

Whilst the commercial harvest is low in volume, it is high in value as Australia has an excellent international reputation for quality.

See the Australian Government Fisheries Research & Development Corporation website for more information, www.frdc.com.au.

Commercial horticulture

Australia's size enables it to produce a vast range of fruit and vegetables from tropical zone exotics to temperate staples, from soft fruit, apples in (Victoria, NSW and Tasmania) to banana plantations in (Queensland) and advanced hydroponics.

Australia is largely self-sufficient in fresh fruit and vegetables and most of its exports are to Asian markets. The constant concern over water supplies and the environment has encouraged movement to crop systems where water losses and chemical application can be reduced. There are also opportunities in advanced systems for crop traceability and labelling.

Chapter 14: Oil and Gas Opportunities in Australia

The upstream oil and gas industry is expected to grow at two to three times the rate of the economy for at least the next 15 to 20 years. Services to the oil and gas industry are expected to grow even faster in the wake of the new wave of outsourcing by energy companies.

Australia, and particularly Western Australia, is well placed to play a greater global and regional role in the current cycle. A new era heralds changes that provide opportunities for existing players and new players entering the industry. Many of the mega trends underpinning the current cycle are in Western Australia. The major technology change at the exploration and extraction end of the chain is the move to deep water and growth in associated subsea technologies. Most of the current and proposed mega-projects off Western Australia and the Northern Territory require these technologies.

The demand by energy companies for a more integrated and seamless product offering across the full asset lifecycle from engineering through to maintenance modifications and operations potentially provides the greatest opportunities for UK companies to partner with Australian companies.

The growth of the integrated service model potentially offers additional opportunities for niche players in areas such as education and training, health and safety and environmental services. A number of international service providers are either acquiring or developing this expertise in-house or forming joint ventures or alliances with specialist providers of high value technical services such as environmental and training services.

A new era in the development of natural gas reserves have just emerged in Western Australia. In 2009 the A$43 billion Gorgon LNG Development was granted State and Federal Government approval. This LNG project has provided a record boost in the value of minerals and energy projects in Australia. The value of those projects was $112.5 billion as of October 2009, an increase of 40 per cent since April of that year.

There are 74 projects under construction or which have had funding committed - 38 Energy, 31 Minerals and five mineral processing projects. Western Australia is the nation's primary petroleum producer, accounting for 73 per cent of natural gas and 64 per cent of crude oil and condensate production. The State's petroleum industry is the second most valuable resource sector after iron ore. The Western Australia Department of Mines and Petroleum estimates that by 2015, projected expenditure for major gas-related projects in Western Australia will exceed A$148 billion.

The Bass Strait, between Victoria and Tasmania, has the most mature pipeline system within. The region has been a critical building block underpinning the economic growth of the nation producing almost two-thirds of Australia's cumulative oil production to date and 30 per cent of Australia's gas production. There is significant oil supply and approximately seven trillion cubic feet of gas reserves remaining in the basin.

Major Commenced or Committed Projects:

Pyrenees oil development in the Exmouth sub-basin (BHP Billiton)
1. The North West Shelf Venture (Woodside Energy).
2. Greater Gorgon Development (Chevron)
3. Darwin LNG plant (ConocoPhillips)
4. Pluto LNG Project (Woodside)
5. Devil Creek Development Project (Apache)
6. Otway Gas Project (Woodside)
7. Basker-Manta Oil Project (Anzon)
8. Casino Gas Project (Santos)
9. Turrum Oil and Gas Field (Exxon Mobil)

Projects Under Consideration:
1. Ichthys LNG Project (Inpex). In FEED stage.
2. Macedon Gas Field (BHP Billiton). Construction expected to start end 2010.
3. Pilbara-Wheatstone LNG Development (Chevron). FID planned mid 2011.
4. Kimberley Browse LNG Development (Woodside) Development options for the Torosa, Brecknock and Calliance fields.

Final Investment Decision planned end 2012. In the wake of a new wave of outsourcing by operators, services to the oil and gas industry are expected to grow even faster.

Two major growth themes are apparent:

The provision of 'life of asset services' from engineering through to maintenance; and Deep-water technology products and services.

For engineering services there are significant opportunities at the front end of the asset development cycle for LNG facilities. The subsea sector is a major growth segment in which global expenditure is forecast to increase from US$61 billion over the five years to 2010, to US$85 billion for the five years 2010-2015. Western Australia has become important equipment and services provider for the oil and gas sector across Australia and into South East Asia and is supported by a substantial and growing research and training industry.

A number of major international companies have relocated their regional operations and administrative bases to Perth. They have joined local firms in providing a comprehensive supply and service capacity and are major contributors to the State's economy.

Western Australian based firms have participated in the development of the State's multi-billion dollar LNG industry over the past two decades. As a result, they have had to meet and exceed the exacting engineering and quality assurance standards required for offshore and onshore construction, repairs and maintenance.

The local supply and service sector also provides exploration and information analysis services, advanced software development, skilled maritime and drilling crews, supply vessels and sub-sea services.

Business costs are lower compared with neighbouring countries. Taxation and royalty arrangements in place are internationally competitive. The policy and legal framework for oil and gas development is attractive and conducive to companies of all sizes. Sovereign risk is low. Regulatory requirements are transparent, predictable and practical, covering all stages of operations.

Chapter 15: Marine Industry Opportunities in Australia

Australia's marine industry is renowned for its innovation, design capabilities and quality workmanship. The marine industry is growing again after being negatively affected by the Global Financial Crisis. There are low barriers to entry and boating is very much an important component of the Australian recreational lifestyle.

The Australian marine industry can be broken down into a range of products and services that fit into recreational, commercial and defence activities. The Australian marine industry includes:
1. Ship/boat-building and repair
2. Marine equipment manufacturing
3. Marina services and operations
4. Marine retail products
5. Yacht and Super yacht building, refit and services

The industry is an important contributor to the Australian economy. Industry turnover is around A$5.5 billion, consists of 2700 companies and employs over 29,000 people.

Marine equipment retailers sell a broad range of boats, outboard motors, boat trailers and accessories. These products are purchased from domestic and international wholesalers. Operators then retail these goods, through their stores to the general public for private use.

Industry outlook

Industry sales are expected to rise by 2.3% per annum, and will continue to be affected by trends in real household disposable income, coastal population levels, interest rates and leisure time availability. Increasing levels of competition from internal players will also heightened trading conditions for retailers over this period. Retail demand for marine equipment will also be driven by trends in real household disposable income which is expected to rise 3.6% per annum over the five years to 2014-15.

Following a decline in income levels in 2009-10 (due to the lack of a Federal Government handout compared to 2008-09); income levels will post growth in 2010-11, peaking in 2011-12 with growth of 4.6%. Income growth will stem from rising wages and job numbers as the economy recovers. However, retail spending levels will be affected by rising interest rates over the five years to 2014-15 as the economy enters its next expansionary phase. Overall, the volatile nature of interest rates over the next five years will have notable repercussions for the luxury end of marine equipment.

International Trade

International trade in marine equipment is largely conducted at the manufacturing or wholesale level and generally not regarded an activity of this industry to avoid double counting. Over the past five years, the industry has experienced repeated concerns by manufacturers and retailers regarding the number of boats being imported into Australia. This tends to suggest that while the industry performs well, it is busy selling imported boats which are affecting local manufacturers, with their share of the local market reported to have declined by 50%. As a result, the boat manufacturing industry has had to strive to achieve a healthy share of the local market and also focus on the export market for its survival.

The 4 major players in boat sales are Fairline, Sunseeker and Princess all UK companies. At the export level, Australia is regarded as a significant exporter of boats and marine equipment. Marine industry exports amount to around $500.0 million in 2004 and exports rose to about $620.0 million in 2005 and are reported to have reached $750.0 million in crafts and marine products exported to a range of countries including New Zealand, the Pacific Rim, USA, Europe, South America and the Caribbean.

The marine equipment market has significant potential for future export growth to areas such as Dubai, Malaysia, Korea and China. Growth in demand for Australian marine exports has been fuelled by the success and popularity of Australian goods at international trade shows.

Marine exports in Australia are overseen by the Australian International Marine Export Group (AIMEX). Established in 1998, AIMEX is a representative body of members from Australia's recreational and light commercial boating industry, boat manufacturers, suppliers of marine goods and services along with the Australian Marine Industries Federation.

AIMEX has been established to develop and promote the competitiveness of Australia in boating and marine products by developing an internationally recognised brand image.

Current laws require that boats purchased by international buyers be exported within 60 days of purchase to quality for GST-free status. As part of the Federal Budget 2010, the government has proposed that the export date be extended to witin12 months of purchase, provided that the boat is only used for recreational use whilst in Australia. Following unanimous agreement by state and territory governments, the changes came into effect in 2011.

Australia is designed for boating. With a coastline of 59 000km and 85 per cent of the population living within 50km of the coast, it is natural that boating has become a part of the Australian psyche and recreational lifestyle. Furthermore, as one of the few developed economies to not go into recession in recent years, Australians have more disposable income relative to many other developed markets. The Australian Bureau of Statistics confirmed that in the ten years to 2009, Australians had increased their real disposable income by 2.6 per cent per year. Growth in the marine industry is predicted at a rate of 2.5 per cent per annum until 2014-15. Australia also has one of the highest boat ownership rates in the world, with 750 000 registered leisure craft in a country with a population of about 22 million.

State imposed barriers to entry into the Australian market are relatively low. Customs duties on marine goods originating in Britain range from 0-5%. However, it must be noted that there is virtually no product or service available that is not already represented in the Australian marine industry.

Boat-building and Marine Equipment Retail

Of the entire revenue generated by the marine industry in Australia, the boat-building and marine equipment retail sectors contribute A$1 billion and A$2.6 billion respectively.

In recent times the Australian manufacturers have been under increasing pressure from foreign competition as the high Australian currency has given a competitive advantage to firms exporting into the Australian market. Local manufacturers have lost 50% of their market share to international sellers.

Many Australian companies are in the process of streamlining and cutting costs in order to stay viable in the short term until the affects of the Global Financial Crisis abate. This leaves an opportunity for foreign manufacturers to explore the market with weakened local competition. Foreign imports into Australia from the boat-building sector now account for $467 million worth of sales. The United States being the biggest exponent at 38% followed by the UK with 15% or A$78 million.

The majority of marine establishments are located in the warmer states that also have more developed water tourism. Queensland, New South Wales and Western Australia together represent about 80% of marine industry establishments.

A great opportunity for boatbuilding enterprises is the changing demographics of the Australian marine market. Currently the 'baby boomer' generation is entering retirement age. With this is a notable trend for retirees to retire along the coast and hence they engage in marine activities, boosting marine sales. Additionally, 'baby-boomers' generally possess a higher level of disposable income, which bodes well for the marine industry.

The weak growth in income post-GFC may produce growth in aluminium boat sales over fibreglass models. It has also influenced an increase in used boat consumption over new boats.

There are 5 product segments in the Australian boatbuilding sector. Powerboats make up the majority of sales at 45% of sector revenue. Catamarans and Yachts make up approximately 20% of industry revenue with small runabouts and "person-powered" watercraft making up the remainder of the industry revenue figures.

Australian marine industry associations that represent differing fields and their interests include:
1. The Department of Innovation, Industry, Science and Research www.innovation.gov.au
2. The Australian International Marine Export Group (AIMEX) www.aimex.asn.au

3. Australian Marine Industries Federation (AMIF) www.amif.asn.au
4. Australian Shipbuilders Association (ASA) www.shipbuilders.com.au
5. Australian Ship Repairers Group (ASRG) www.asrg.asn.au
6. Marina Industries Association of Australia (MIAA) www.marinas.net.au
7. Super Yacht Base Australia (SYBA) www.superyachtbase.com

Chapter 16: Healthcare Opportunities in Australia

The Australian Healthcare Industry currently generates revenue of AU$94 billion (£60 billion) per year. This is forecast to rise to $108 billion (£70 billion) within the next 5 years.

A recent BMI report rated Australia as the best place in the Asia Pacific region to do business in the Healthcare market, based on market size, structure and risk, ahead of Japan, Korea and China (as well as Singapore and India). With beneficial exchange rates, a booming economy and proximity to the emerging markets of the Asia Pacific region, there has never been a better time to do business in Australia.

Australia has a strong local manufacturing industry but is still a net importer of medicines, medical devices and equipment.

Likewise Australia has a well educated and experienced services sector, but excellence from the UK and NHS is recognised and sort after.

Therefore opportunities exist across the full range of the Australian Healthcare Industry, including:
1. Selling pharmaceuticals, diagnostics, medical equipment and preventative healthcare products.
2. Providing aged, home and community based care services.

3. Providing information technology and software products for the full chain of healthcare management.
4. Providing health insurance packages.

Health System Overview

The Australian Health system is run through a combination of Commonwealth and State government management. The Commonwealth currently has a leadership role in policy making and particularly in national issues like public health, research and national information management.

The States and Territories are primarily responsible for the delivery and management of public health services and for maintaining direct relationships with most healthcare providers. The States and Territories deliver public acute and psychiatric hospital services and a wide range of community and public health services.

The State and Territory governments directly fund a broad range of health services. The Commonwealth funds most medical services out of hospital and most health research. The Commonwealth, States and Territories jointly fund public hospitals and community care for aged and disabled persons.

National Healthcare Funding System The aim of the national healthcare funding system is to give universal access to healthcare while allowing choice for individuals through a substantial private sector involvement in delivery and financing. The major part of the funding system is called "Medicare". Medicare provides high quality health care which is both affordable and accessible to all Australians, often provided free of charge at the point of care.

It is financed largely from general taxation revenue, which includes a Medicare levy based on a person's taxable income. Commonwealth funding for Medicare is mainly provided as Subsidies for prescribed medicines (with a safety net providing free medicines for the chronically ill) and free or subsidised treatment by practitioners such as doctors, participating optometrists or dentists; Substantial grants to State and Territory governments to contribute to the costs of providing access to public hospitals at no cost to patients; and Specific purpose grants to State/Territory governments and other bodies.

In addition, Commonwealth general purpose funding grants to State and Territory governments flow partly to health services. State and Territory governments supplement Medicare funding with their own revenues, mainly for funding public hospitals. Proposed Changes to the National Health Reform Agreement was signed by the Commonwealth, State and Territory governments on 2nd August 2011.

Under this Agreement the Commonwealth will fund half the efficient cost of delivering public hospital services. The Agreement is also designed to form a greater link between Commonwealth and State health systems by removing layers of government and the forming of two new forms of local management,

Medicare Locals for Primary Health and Local Hospital Networks for Public Hospitals.

National Health Reform will:
1. Invest an additional $19.8 billion in public hospital services over this decade.
2. Reduce waiting times for emergency departments.
3. Ensure all patients receive elective surgery on time.
4. Allow all Australians to see how their hospitals and Medicare Locals are performing.
5. Give local communities and clinicians a greater say in the delivery of local services.

The National Health Reform Agreement will ensure that there are more streamlined, collaborative, flexible and transparent funding processes through the creation of a single National Health Funding Pool. An Administrator will oversee both Commonwealth and state and territory funding of the public hospital system. Payments will be made from the Pool to Local Hospital Networks using a nationally consistent approach to activity based funding.

The National Health Funding Pool will be operational by 1 July 2012 and be administered by an independent Administrator who will be distinct from Commonwealth, state and territory government departments.

Public hospital services will be provided under service agreements negotiated between each Local Hospital Network and the respective state or territory government. State and territory governments will also be responsible for providing system-wide service planning and performance management including disseminating best practice, and identifying and remediating poor performance.

Local Hospital Networks will also work with the new Medicare Locals (which are responsible for coordinating local primary health care delivery) to identify and address particular local needs and to ensure continuity of care for patients between hospital and primary health care services.

Medicare Locals will work to support integrated and coordinated primary health care services (such as general practices, community health centres and allied health services) to keep people well and out of hospital and ensure that all Australians have access to effective and accessible after hours care. Medicare Locals are already being established and will be established throughout Australia by July 2012.

The primary role of Medicare Locals will relate to service coordination and planning, with service delivery as a secondary function where required. Medicare Locals will be able to identify gaps in services at the local level and examine opportunities for better targeting of services, working collaboratively with Local Hospital Networks and aged care service providers.

The Commonwealth Government considers that strong private sector involvement in health services provision and financing is essential to the viability of the Australian health system. For this reason the Commonwealth Government provides a 30 per cent subsidy to individuals who acquire private health insurance and has introduced additional arrangements to foster lifelong participation in private health insurance.

Costs incurred by patients receiving private doctors' services and some optometrical services and dental surgery, whether in or out of hospital, are generally reimbursed either fully or in part by means of Medicare benefits.

Private hospitals make up around 22% of all hospitals in Australia. Private hospitals are owned by for-profit or not-for-profit organisations such as large corporate operators, religious operators and private health insurance funds.

The two largest for-profit hospital operators are Ramsay Health Care and Health scope who account for about 40% of all private hospital beds in Australia between them.

Medicines/Pharmaceuticals

The Pharmaceutical Benefits Scheme (PBS) aims to provide all Medicare-eligible persons with access to effective and necessary prescription medications at a reasonable cost to the patients and to the nation.

The PBS provides subsidies for about 600 kinds of drugs in nearly 1500 formulations which means patients can obtain reasonably priced medicines for most medical conditions.

State funded administrative regions generally have centralised purchasing departments that look after the purchasing of some items for all the institutions under their jurisdiction. For major new facilities or some product supplies they will offer tenders to interested suppliers.

A similar arrangement is seen at major privately owned healthcare providers like hospital operators, general practitioner companies or pathology laboratories. Other products such as medicines, devices and general medical supplies may be sold directly to individual facilities or even patients.

In most cases it would be imperative to have a local presence to be able to communicate directly with government bodies, key health decision makers or patients.

Chapter 17: Business Risk

Bribery and Corruption

Bribery is illegal. It is an offence for British nationals or someone who is ordinarily resident in the UK, a body incorporated in the UK or a Scottish partnership, to bribe anywhere in the world.

In addition, a commercial organisation carrying on a business in the UK can be liable for the conduct of a person who is neither a UK national or resident in the UK or a body incorporated or formed in the UK. In this case it does not matter whether the acts or omissions which form part of the offence take place in the UK or elsewhere.

According to the Transparency International's corruption perception index, (CPI) Australia ranked 8th in 2009, 9th in 2008, 11th in 2007, and 9th in 2006. This means the perceived level of corruption in Australia is comparable to Sweden, Finland, Denmark, Switzerland and Canada.

Visit the Business Anti-Corruption portal which provides advice and guidance about corruption in overseas markets.

In December 2010 a Supreme Court jury convicted three men resident in Melbourne of conspiring to plan a terrorist attack. They had been arrested in 2009, while plotting to attack the Holsworthy army barracks in Sydney with firearms.

In November 2005, the Australian police arrested 16 people in Sydney and Melbourne in a counter-terrorism operation designed to disrupt preparations for a terrorist attack. Three more were arrested on terrorism charges in Melbourne in March 2006. The trial against those arrested in Melbourne concluded on 15 September 2008 with six convictions and four acquittals. The case against those from Sydney concluded on 16 October 2009 with five convictions.

Like in any country it is important to take precautions for individual and business security when doing business in Australia. However, on the whole the threat in Australia is no greater than in the UK.

Intellectual Property

IP protection in Australia is strong and an important consideration for UK businesses looking to do business in Australia. Under common law the principal forms of intellectual property protection available in Australia are trademarks, designs, patents and copyright.

All of these forms of protection are governed by legislation. The common law also provides remedies against a person passing off goods or services as those of another, as well as protection for confidential information or trade secrets.

Organised Crime

As in many other major countries, international organised criminal activity takes place in parts of

Australia, in particular linked to drugs, people smuggling and people trafficking.

Chapter 18: Political Overview

Australia has a system of Government based on liberal democratic values of religious tolerance, freedom of speech and association, and the rule of law. Australia has similar political, legal and regulatory practices to the UK, the USA and other liberal democracies.

The Australian Constitution of 1901 established a federal system of government. Under this system, powers are distributed between a federal government (the Commonwealth) and the six States.

Two Territories - the Australian Capital Territory and the Northern Territory - have more limited powers; there are also a number of offshore territories, of which the most significant are Norfolk Island and the Australian Antarctic Territory. The Parliament is at the heart of the Australian government. The Parliament consists of The Queen (represented by the Governor-General) and two Houses: the Senate and the House of Representatives. Australia is thus a constitutional monarchy, a federation and a parliamentary democracy.

The 43rd Australian Parliament was sworn in by the Governor-General on 28 September 2010, after a general election was held on 21 August resulting in a hung Parliament. The Australian Labour Party (ALP), led by Julia Gillard, formed a minority government, with the support of three independent MPs and the one Green party MP. The 43rd Australian Parliament has introduced a number of Parliamentary reforms and includes the first Indigenous Member of Parliament.

Members of the House of Representatives (Lower House) serve three-year terms. Senators serve fixed six-year terms (from 1 July). It is usual to hold a full House of Representatives and a half-Senate election simultaneously every three years.

It is important to note that laws and regulatory practices can change between Australia states, so businesses looking to operate in multiple Australian states should check the regulations in each state.

The federal Australian Labour Party's election victory in November 2007 saw wall-to-wall Labour governments across Australia until a closely fought State election in August 2008 saw the Western Australian Liberal Party form a government with support from the National Party and an independent, led by Colin Barnett. In March 2009, Anna Bligh led the Queensland Labour Party to a third successive election victory.

David Bartlett was re-elected Premier of Tasmania, leading a Labour-Greens coalition after a closely fought election in March 2010. Ted Baillieu, Liberal Party, was sworn in as Victoria's Premier in December 2010, following 11 years of Labour Governments. Barry O'Farrell, Liberal Party, was elected as Premier of NSW following the March 2011 state election. Jay Weatherill replaced Mike Rann, as leader of the Labour Party and South Australia's Premier in October 2011.

The Liberal Party currently hold power in three of eight states and territories.

Indigenous Aboriginal Community

The treatment of the indigenous Aboriginal community (2.4% of the population) has challenged successive Australian governments. A central point of the Labour Government's 2007 election campaign was to address the challenges facing the indigenous population. On the first day of the new Australian Parliament in February 2008, then Prime Minister Kevin Rudd made a formal apology on behalf of the government to Australia's indigenous population for the treatment of the 'Stolen Generation' (government-backed schemes between 1920 and 1970 to remove Aboriginal and Torres Strait Islander children from their parents and place them with white families).

Republic Debate

In a constitutional referendum held on 6 November 1999, Australia voted to remain a constitutional monarchy (55% to 45%). Voters were offered a choice between the status quo and the republican model approved by the 1998 Constitutional Convention: a President appointed by a two-thirds majority in Parliament. Republicans wanting a directly elected president formed an unlikely coalition with monarchists to defeat the referendum. Despite the result, there is extensive republican sentiment in Australia. The Australian Labour Party supports a republic. Tony Abbott, leader of the opposition, is a well known supporter of the Monarchy.

Chapter 19: Australia Fact File

Australia's political and regulatory environment is stable, open and progressive, providing business with a high degree of confidence and certainty.

Australia's political system is highly effective in responding to economic challenges and policy direction. The adaptability of Australian government policy to changes in the economy has been ranked in the top four countries in the region (source: IMD World Competitiveness Yearbook 2011). Similarly, the transperancy and effectiveness of government are also rated highly (source: Ibid).

The current federal Labour Government, led by Prime Minister Julia Gillard, has shown a strong commitment to providing businesses with the right conditions for growth and trade. Trade liberalisation and reductions in tarriff barriers in recent years has resulted in strong productivity and enabled businesses to be highly responsive to economic conditions.

Australia is about the same geographical size as continental USA, but with a much smaller population of 22.6 million, mostly concentrated on the east coast.

Australia's international airline QANTAS regularly co-shares with British Airways and many other major international carriers operate regular flights to Australia.

The peak season for travel to and from Australia is October to February mid-spring and summer in the southern hemisphere. If you travel during Australia's winter and early spring (June through September) you might save as much as 50 per cent.

Distance and travel time from the UK varies slightly. For example: Air distance between Manchester and Sydney is 16,972.1km (10,546 miles) and takes 21 hrs 54mins.

Air distance between London and Perth is 14,419.2km (8,959.7 miles) and takes 18hrs 36mins.

Travel within Australian cities is reasonably easy via rail, bus, ferry, tram and taxi but if you want to travel outside the metropolitan areas, it is best to hire a car.

Australia has three time zones, with some states observing daylight savings time and others not. Over 664,000 British Nationals visit Australia every year most without incident.

Australia occupies the whole of the island continent of the same name and lies between the Indian and Pacific Oceans. Although the country's land mass is half as big again as that of Europe, most of Australia is empty.

The population is predominantly concentrated in the south eastern coastal cities of Sydney, Brisbane, Melbourne and Adelaide. The interior of the country - the Outback - is comprised of sparsely populated semi-desert and tropical wetlands.

Area: 7,682m sq km
Population: 22.7 million
Capital city: Canberra
People: 98% of the population are of European or Asian descent.

Languages:

Mainly English with some other European, indigenous and Asian languages

Religion(s):

Majority Christian with Buddhist, Jewish, Muslim and other minorities; in the 2006 Census, 18.7% of the population defined themselves as having "no religion". Freedom of religion is guaranteed by the constitution.

Currency:

Australian Dollar (A$)

Major political parties:

The main national political parties are the Australian Labour Party (ALP), Liberal Party, National Party, and the Australian Greens. The Liberal and National Parties are in coalition at the national level, and in most states; in Queensland, they merged in 1998 to form the Liberal National Party, while in the Northern Territory they merged in 1975 to form the Country Liberal Party.

Membership of international groups/organisations:

The United Nations (UN), the Commonwealth, the World Trade Organisation (WTO), the Asia Pacific Economic Co-operation (APEC), Organisation for Economic Cooperation and Development (OECD), the ASEAN Regional Forum (ARF), East Asia Summit (EAS), United Nations Educational, Scientific and Cultural Organisation (UNESCO), Pacific Islands Forum (PIF), the Group of 20 (G20), the Major Economies Forum (MEF).

Chapter 20: Economic Overview

Australia has had one of the best-performing economies in the industrialised world in recent decades. It has not suffered a recession for the past 19 years. This success reflects many factors, including sound economic management, strong population growth, a rich endowment of natural resources (particularly mining) and close ties to the boom economies of Asia.

But the country faces a number of challenges. The economy is already hitting capacity limits; particularly labour shortages and these are expected to worsen due to the mining boom. And due to its carbon intensive economy, Australia is the largest per capita emitter of greenhouses gases in the developed world.

Economic Outlook

Australia's economic prospects appear strong, thanks in large part to the mining boom. Soaring prices for iron ore, coal, gold and liquefied natural gas (LNG) have provided a significant income injection into the economy. A mining investment boom is underway in resource-rich states like Western Australia and Queensland.

Official interest rates have already started rising from a 'neutral' to a 'restrictive' setting, albeit slowly. Unemployment is low and labour is in short supply in many industries and regions. The mining boom is expected to fuel these inflationary pressures. The boom has pushed the Australian dollar to record highs. The high dollar is hurting trade-exposed sectors like manufacturing and tourism.

Key Economic indicators

GDP: A$1.2 trillion

GDP growth: Year to June 2011: 1.4 per cent

Inflation (CPI):   2.8% (year to June 2010)

Unemployment: 5.1% (September 2010)

Aid and development: The 2010-11 overseas development assistance (ODA) budget is A$4.4bn (US$3.7bn), representing 0.33% of GNI. The government is committed to raising this to 0.5% of GNI by 2015-16.

Australia's status as an advanced market economy is reflected in its membership, since 1971, of the Organisation for Economic Cooperation and Development (OECD). It is the 13th largest economy in the world by nominal GDP (the 18th largest when GDP is adjusted to take account of purchasing power). In 2009, it was the world's 21st biggest exporter and 23rd biggest importer. Per capita GDP is comparable with European economies such as the UK and Germany.

The Australian economy is diversified, with the service sector (including tourism, education, financial services and information and communications technology (ICT)) accounting for 68% of GDP. Exports are dominated (57%) by minerals and agricultural products. Though these sectors directly account for only 10% of GDP, strong growth in minerals exports, primarily to Asian markets, has played a key role in Australia's near two decades of continuous economic expansion and in its weathering of the global financial crisis of 2008-09. Key agricultural exports include coal, iron ore, gold, aluminium, liquefied natural gas (LNG) meat, wheat and wool.

Australia navigated the global financial crisis in better shape than most other advanced economies. Its economy proved resilient, thanks in part to fiscal and monetary stimulus measures, the strength of the banking sector, and continued Chinese demand for Australian minerals. Despite the worst global financial and economic crisis in 75 years, when most advanced economies contracted, the Australian economy not only continued to grow, but grew steadily, with GDP growing by 1.4 per cent in 2009, compared to a 3.2 per cent contraction among advanced economies.

Australia's reputation as a highly competitive economy continues to strengthen. In the IMD World Competitiveness Yearbook 2011 Australia ranks number 9, just behind Hong Kong, Singapore, USA, Sweden, Switzerland, Taiwan, Canada, and Qatar, placing it in the top four countries in the Asia-Pacific for its overall competitiveness.

Among countries with a population of 20 million or more, Australia ranks third in the world, behind only the United States and Canada. (source: IMD, World Competitiveness Yearbook, 2011).

This, together with a strong and independent financial sector and an effective and proven regulatory system means Australia provides a sound trading partner for British business. Harvard Business Review named Australia as its No. 1 country to invest in Jan/Feb 2011.

Australia's exposure to and engagement with the Asian region which still has the most dynamic growth potential in the world, offers a strategic advantage to companies looking to position themselves for global growth opportunities.

Population and territory

Australia covers 7.68 million km², and has a population of 22.6 million (at July 2011 – source: www.abs.gov.au).
Population by city (2007):
Sydney – 4.58 million
Melbourne – 4 million
Brisbane – 2 million
Perth – 1.6 million
Adelaide – 1.2 million
Canberra (Capital City) - 0.35 million

Sydney and Melbourne are Australia's largest cities and principal commercial centres. Brisbane, Adelaide and Perth offer important export opportunities as well across a diverse range of industries. Canberra has little manufacturing industry, however there is much activity centred on federal administration of government departments and authorities.

Chapter 21: International Trade

Australia's trade is increasingly directed towards Asia. The country's biggest two-way trading partner is China, followed by Japan, the US, Republic of Korea and the UK. Biggest exports are coal and iron ore, followed by education services and gold. The terms of trade are near a record high due to surging commodities prices.

Australia is a strong proponent of trade liberalisation. But with progress in the Doha round of trade talks slow, it has entered free trade agreements with New Zealand, Thailand, Chile, the US and the Association of South East Asian Nations (ASEAN). It is also negotiating FTAs with China, Malaysia and Japan, as well as three regional deals. Although agricultural tariffs are very low compared to other developed countries, Australia is sometimes accused of using its strict quarantine regime as a trade barrier.

Rich in natural resources, Australia has a largely affluent society and an open and innovative economy, resulting in growing foreign investment over the past decade. Australia continues to be a strong advocate of increased trade liberalisation in the World Trade Organisation and plays an active role in global trade talks.

Strong political, economic and cultural links to the UK make Australia a more significant market for UK exports than its comparatively small population might suggest. The UK is Australia's fifth largest two-way trading partner, worth A$22.6 billion in 2010. British investment in Australia increased A$34 billion in 2009 to reach A$499 billion, making the UK the country's second biggest foreign investor after the US. And it is second largest foreign direct investor, worth with A$63 billion, or 14.5 per cent of the total. Despite the global economic slowdown, UK foreign direct investment into Australia increased by A$1.8 billion in the year to December 2009.

The UK sells more to Australia than to India or China, and Australia is the UK's 5th largest market for goods outside the EU. Agriculture, mining, oil and gas, environment and green technology, financial and professional services, information and communication technology, biotechnology, education, creative and media, marine, railways, food and drink, recreation and leisure, defence, and aerospace are all sectors identified as offering significant opportunities for British companies.

The UK is also a major partner for Australia's trade in services. In 2009, it was Australia's third largest market for services exports, worth A$4.2 billion, and second largest source for services imports, worth A$4.9 billion. Trade in services between the two countries contracted modestly due to the global financial crisis, but is expected to rebound in 2012. On both sides, recreational travel remains the strongest contributor to services trade.

Australia's trade policy is geared to increasing economic activity, liberalising trade and maximising access for Australia in the international market place. Australia is an active player in the WTO, in particular on agriculture. Australia is actively pursuing regional and bilateral free trade agreements, which, it hopes, will deliver stronger trade and economic growth.

FTA's have been completed with the US, Singapore, Thailand, New Zealand, Chile and ASEAN, and negotiations are underway with China, Malaysia, Japan, Korea, the Gulf Cooperation Council, Pacific islands (through the Pacific Agreement on Closer economic Relations) and the Trans Pacific Partnership. Further bilateral FTA's with India and Indonesia are also under consideration.

Chapter 22: International Relations

Foreign policy

Australia maintains close ties with Europe and North America, and has a history of active engagement throughout Asia and the Pacific. Australia has long-standing security and intelligence relationships with the US and UK. In 2011 Prime Minister Julia Gillard announced the development of a White Paper titled "Australia in the Asian Century". Gillard said that Australia would seek a peaceful rules-based Asia, effective regional institutions, with "space for a rising China, and a robust US-Australia alliance".

Australia supports continued US strategic engagement in Asia as an essential contribution to regional stability and prosperity and their bilateral relationship is underpinned by the recent announcement during President Obama's visit of US troop deployment plans in Northern Australia. In recent years Australia has worked hard diplomatically to strengthen its links with the EU and in October 2008 the EU-Australia Partnership Framework was launched. Close engagement with its Asian neighbours is a high priority in Australian foreign and trade policy.

The Australian Government pays particular attention to building a strategic economic partnership with China and is engaged in negotiating a Free Trade Agreement. In 2007 Australia hosted the APEC

Summit in Sydney. Australia has established human rights dialogues with China, Vietnam and Burma.

Australia is seeking election as a non-permanent member of the UN Security Council from 2013.

Security

In its immediate neighbourhood Australia is helping to restore sound governance and political stability to the Solomon Islands through its primary role in RAMSI (Regional Assistance Mission to the Solomon Islands), Timor-Leste as the largest contributor to Operation Astute (in support of the UNMIT mission) and Papua New Guinea through the bilateral Defence Cooperation Programme. It currently has approximately 685 Australian Defence Force (ADF) and Australian Federal Police (AFP) personnel deployed in these three countries.

Further afield, Australia deploys up to 1550 ADF personnel in Afghanistan as part of the NATO-led International Stabilisation and Assistance Force (ISAF).This deployment is primarily in Oruzgan Province with the focus on mentoring Afghan security forces and assisting with reconstruction.

Australia withdrew its combat troops from Iraq in mid 2008 and now only has two officers to provide local security for the Australian Embassy. In summary, approximately 3,300 ADF personnel are deployed overseas to protect Australia and its national interests, with a further 400 involved in maritime protection around its coastline. Approximately 300

AFP personnel are deployed overseas and across Australia's external territories.

The Defence White Paper published on 2 May 2009 set out the future size and force structure of the ADF. This was amplified by the publication on 1 July 2009 of the Defence Capability Plan (DCP), which set out the Department's equipment spending plans over the coming four year Forward Estimates period. The funding for this programme (A$104bn) will be supplemented by the Defence Strategic Reform Programme (SRP), which envisages savings of A$20bn over the next 10 years. The February 2010 publication 'The Strategic Reform Programme – Making it Happen' set out some changes to the DCP and the Budget for FY 2010-11 confirmed both the Government's commitment to defence and the key importance of the SRP's cost reduction plans in enabling a reasonably ambitious budget.

In September 2011 the second UK-Australia Defence Policy Talks and the Strategic Dialogue meeting were held in London at 3* level, setting the top level context and framework for the UK-Australian defence and foreign policy relationship.

Defence

The relationship between our respective Armed Forces remains stronger than ever, particularly as a result of recent and ongoing deployment operations together.

Following the drawdown of ADF personnel from Iraq, both countries remain strongly committed to operations in Afghanistan, where the ADF contribution continues to be capped at 1,550. There is also a significant personnel exchange programme backed up by numerous mutual training and educational opportunities that continue to be reviewed and expanded upon.

The UK and Australia are members of the Five Power Defence Arrangement (FPDA – UK, Australia, Singapore, Malaysia and New Zealand) and the America, Britain, Canada, Australia and New Zealand (ABCA) Interoperability Programme, and routinely exercise together under one of these two agreements. Australia continues to be an important market for UK defence exports.

Climate change

Australia is the 15th largest emitter of greenhouse gases, accounting for 1.48% of total global emissions. On a per capita basis, it is the world's largest emitter (excepting small oil-based economies such as the Gulf States), producing more greenhouse gases per head than even the United States. This reflects, in part, its reliance on coal-fired power stations for electricity. Between 1990 and 2006, Australia's emissions grew by over 21% (source: World Resources Institute).

Australia signed the Kyoto Protocol, an international agreement to reduce greenhouse gas emissions, in 1997, but declined to ratify it until after the election of the new Labour government in 2007 With the passage of the Clean Energy Future package through the Senate on 8 November, Australia becomes only the second country outside the EU to legislate a statutory, economy-wide emissions trading scheme. The legislation establishes a fixed price on carbon from July 2012, transitioning to a fully-fledged economy-wide emissions trading scheme in 2015. Australia is investing substantial sums in research and development in solar energy and carbon capture and storage (CCS), and hosts the Global CCS Institute.

Science and Innovation

Australia has a strong Science and Innovation community. With only 0.3% of the world's population it accounts for 2.9% of the world's scientific publications and 2.5% of the global medical research. With one third of all Australian scientific publications having at least one overseas co-author, Australia can be classed as very outward looking. The USA is Australia's largest scientific partner but it also has strong scientific relationships with China and India (Source: DIISR).

Traditionally Australia's research strengths have been in the areas of science best complementing its natural resources and geographical endowments, for example; engineering, technology sciences, agricultural and environmental sciences and the biological and earth sciences. However Australia also has a solid presence in emerging fields such as photonics and biotechnology.

Chapter 23: UK Australia People Facts

Passports

Since June 2009 all UK passports from Australia are issued from the Regional Passport Processing Centre (RPPC) in New Zealand. The RPPC issues approximately 90000 UK passports a year with 65000 going to Australia.

Further details on acquiring UK passports can be found at: http://ukinnewzealand.fco.gov.uk/en/help-for-british-nationals/passports/how-to-apply/australia

Visas

More than 95% of visits to the UK from Australia are visa free. In the 12 months between April 2008 and April 2009, the British High Commission in Canberra issued 27,584 visas, a fall of 10% or 3,173 on the previous year largely because of the global economic downturn. Of these, about 13,000 were a combination of working holidaymaker and Tier 5 YMS visas, 2,800 ancestry visas, 1,300 settlement visas, 1,800 work permits, 800 students and 2,000 highly skilled visas.

Travel to the UK

In 2009, approximately 430,800 Australians visited the UK (Source: ABS) compared with 418,400 in 2008.

Travel to Australia

In 2009, approximately 670,800 Britons visited Australia (Source: ABS) compared with 668,200 in 2008. 40,182 Britons were granted working holidaymaker visas for Australia in 2008-09, compared with 34,145 in 2007-08 (source: DIAC). The total number of Britons entering Australia for any purpose in 2008/09 and from any country was 1,285,975 (source: DIAC). Most visits to Australia are trouble–free. 378 British nationals required consular assistance in Australia in the period 1 April 2009 – 31 March 2010 for the following types of incidents: 77 deaths; 42 hospitalisations; and 124 arrests, for a variety of offences.

During this period lost or stolen passports were by far the most frequent problem encountered by British nationals in Australia (980 cases).

Britons Immigrating to Australia

In 2008-09, 21,545 Britons immigrated to Australia. Of these, 15,803 were 'skilled' migrants and 4, 219 were 'family' migrants (Source: DIAC). In addition, several thousand more (probably around 7,000 or so) applied for settlement while they were already within Australia. The figures on settlement are broadly consistent with the previous year. 21,070 Britons were '457' temporary skilled migrants in 2008-09, making the UK the largest source of 457 visa holders.

UK Population in Australia

The number of British-born people in Australia rose slightly between 2001 and 2006 to 1.04m (Source: Australian Census 2006). Of these, 245,000 receive British State pensions (Source: DWP).

Child Migrants

Child Migrants were British children in care, who were sent, under government approved schemes, to certain Commonwealth countries (Canada, Australia, New Zealand, and Rhodesia - now Zimbabwe). These schemes can be traced as far back as 300 years ago and continued until the 1960s. A House of Commons Health Select Committee visited Australia in June 1998 in connection with its inquiry into the welfare of former child migrants. The Committee's report, in July 1998, detailed the stories of many child migrants who had endured physical and sexual abuse, systematic punishment, and separation from siblings.

The British Government responded in December 1998, offering increased funding to the Child Migrants Trust to enable child migrants to visit relatives in the UK. The Government set up a database containing details of child migrants and a website. The Child Migrants Trust has now completed this work.

In June 2000 the Australian Senate Community Affairs Reference Committee agreed to hold an inquiry into the child migration scheme. The

Committee published a report on 30 August, entitled 'Lost Innocents: righting the Record', which contained 33 recommendations - some for the British Government.

The Australian Government responded in 2002 by announcing a package of measures worth A$3.7 million (about £1.3million) to provide practical support and assistance to former child migrants to Australia. In February 2010, the British Prime Minister Gordon Brown issued a formal apology to child migrants, which was echoed during several ceremonies across Australia.

Frozen Pensions

The UK pays about 800,000 pensions overseas. In those countries where no bilateral agreement exists to up-rate pensions, including Australia, they are frozen at the time of migration. 205,000 UK pensioners live in Australia. Of these, 70% qualify for an Australian aged pension, either through residency in Australia, or under the former bilateral social security agreement. In those cases the Australian government pays the difference between the UK frozen rate pension and the Australian aged pension. Australia abrogated the Bilateral Social Security Agreement in 2001.

Existing British pensioners in Australia are not affected; but future British pensioners immigrating to Australia will have to complete the standard 10 years residence before qualifying for an Australian aged pension. Australian pensioners in the UK will be similarly affected. The abrogation also affects entitlements for those travelling between the two countries to welfare payments such as unemployment and invalidity benefits.

Chapter 24: Market Entry

Preparing to Export to Australia

Your company should try to prepare as thoroughly as possible before attempting to export to Australia. This involves developing a clear idea of your goals in the target market, as well as researching what business structure will be most appropriate for establishing in Australia. This should be judged by the varying legal and tax obligations that your business will be subject to.

Companies should consider Australia's geography when assessing business decisions. Compared to the UK, Australia is a vast country with a relatively low population density. It is worth noting that the distance from Sydney to Perth is the same as London to Moscow, and that Brisbane is closer to Melbourne than it is to Cairns (in far north Queensland).

Distances on maps appear small they're not. Decisions on where to base your business and how to expand should be considered carefully; while transport infrastructure is generally good, distribution is an important factor.

Sydney and Melbourne are Australia's largest cities. They are the principal commercial centres. However, Brisbane, Adelaide and Perth offer important export opportunities as well across a diverse range of sectors.

Canberra has little manufacturing industry; however there is much activity centred on Federal administration of government departments and authorities, Parliament House, service based industries.

Start up considerations

A business enterprise in Australia may be operated by a company, a foreign branch, a trust, a joint venture, an individual or a partnership.

The most common forms of operation are establishing an Australian subsidiary by registering an Australian company (which is financially independent from its parent), or by registering as a foreign company. Taxation and legal (liability) obligations differ according to which business structure you intend to operate through. Therefore decisions on business structure should only be made after carefully considering the tax and legal implications of conducting business in Australia.

Establishing an Australian company

Companies fall under the jurisdiction of, and are regulated by, the Corporations Act 2001.The Corporations Act 2001 can be downloaded from the Australian Legal Information Institute (AustLII) at their website www.austlii.edu.au. Once on the website follow Commonwealth resources > Consolidated Acts > Corporations Act. The Australian Securities and Investment Commission (ASIC) is the body responsible for the administration of the Corporations Act and have offices throughout Australai.

Goods and services tax (GST) is a broad-based consumption tax charged at the rate of 10% on the sale of most goods and services and other things in Australia. GST is charged at each step in the supply chain, with registered businesses including GST in the price of goods and services they sell. For GST, a sale or supply includes a sale of goods, lease of premises, hire of equipment, giving advice, export of goods, and supply of other things. A purchase includes an acquisition of goods or services such as trading stock, a lease, consumables and other things.

Chapter 25: Taxation

An Australian resident company is currently subject to tax at a rate of 30 per cent of its taxable income. Taxable income is assessed on the basis of assessable business income less allowable business deductions.

A company is resident in Australia for income tax purposes if it is incorporated in Australia or, if not incorporated in Australia, it carries on business in Australia and either has its central management and control in Australia, or its voting power is controlled by shareholders who are residents of Australia.

A non-resident company is taxed on its Australian source income (apart from interest, dividends, royalties and certain distributions by managed funds, which are subject to withholding tax) at the same rate as a resident company.

Individual income tax

An individual may receive various types of income, including salary and wages, pensions, interest, royalties, partnership and trust distributions and company dividends. The income may have a foreign or an Australian source. A resident of Australia will generally be liable to Australian income tax on income and capital gains derived throughout the world (although there are a number of exceptions).

Australia has entered into bilateral tax treaties with a number of countries to avoid double taxation and prevent fiscal evasion. These agreements are also referred to as 'Double Tax Agreements' or 'Double Tax Conventions'.

The general effect of a tax treaty is to limit Australia's taxing rights in respect of certain types of income derived by a resident of the other country and vice-versa.

Under Australian law, there are different tax rates for residents and non-residents.

Resident individuals pay tax on their taxable income at progressive rates ranging from 0 to 45 per cent. The individual tax rates for 2011/2012 are: (from 1 July 2011)

Each state has a different rate for charging tax on the total payroll of a company. You should check with the Office of State Revenue for the state in which you intend to domicile for the rate appropriate to your operation.

Australia has a compulsory superannuation regime. Employers MUST pay a minimum of 9% of total wages as a superannuation contribution on a quarterly basis, to a fund of the employee's choice. The maximum contribution is $25,000pa for those under the age of 50, or $50,000pa for those over the age of 50. You must establish a default company fund, depending on the size of your operation.

The rules and contribution limits tend to change quite regularly, so please consult your accountant or a wealth management specialist to ensure compliance.

There are some exceptions from the Superannuation Guarantee, including where a Social Security Agreement that Australia has with another country exempts an employee who has been sent to work temporarily in Australia.

Should your staff decide to stay in Australia, they may transfer their UK pensions to Australia and control their pension funds more closely. They should consult wealth management experts to discuss their personal positions.

Accounting

As an Australian company the client will be required to keep proper books and records, prepare an annual financial report, lodge an annual income tax return and also lodge quarterly or monthly business activity statements. The company will also be required to complete an annual return and have this lodged with ASIC.

Wills, Power of Attorney, Guardianship

UK law will prevail in the event of an occurrence that would bring into play a will or power of attorney. However, individuals who move to Australia should reconsider their position, with particular care regarding guardianship of self or dependents. If staff do not have these documents in place, it would be prudent to consult someone in Australia to put them in place.

Life Insurance, Trauma Insurance and Income Protection

It should be noted that by moving to Australia, a company director or employee may void their life insurance. They should consult their advisors in the UK, and potentially engage a specialist in Australia, to ensure continuity of insurance. Particular care should be taken in this process, as continuity of insurance is important, and should the person void their cover in the UK and then not, for some reason, be able to obtain cover in Australia, then they could be putting them and/or their families at risk.

This is also important when considering potential key man insurance and or buy/sell coverage for owners or employees of the business.

Personal Tax Issues for Australia residents Re UK Pensions

Before moving, or definitely within the first six months of moving permanently, staff/you will need to consider what they/you wish to do with your UK pension schemes.

You can transfer your money to a QROPS- Qualifying Registered Overseas Pension Scheme without major tax issues. If you transfer to a non QROPS fund, there are major tax issues. You/your staff should get advice from qualified professionals for this.

Transfers within six months — if you transfer your UK pension to a QROPS within this period, your transfer value will be considered an after-tax (non-concessional) contribution and will count towards your non-concessional contributions cap). An annual cap of $150,000 applies for non-concessional contributions made by an individual into superannuation. A member's fund (under age 65) can receive non-concessional contributions totalling $450,000 in any one financial year provided no further contributions are made in the following two financial years i.e. 1 July to 30 June.

Transfers after six months — if you transfer your UK pension benefit to QROPS after six months, any growth in the value of your pension benefit between the time you became an Australian resident and the time the transfer occurs, is required to be included as assessable income in your Australian tax return for the relevant year of income. It will then be subject to tax at your marginal tax rate (plus Medicare levy).

Living Away from Home allowance (LAFHA)

Living Away from Home allowance (LAFHA) and relocation costs are two excellent ways of ensuring you or your staff has a much cheaper transition to Australia.

The depth and breadth of options available to individuals can range from the tax free income to the equivalent of moving costs, two years rent and other major items. The details are specific to how and what you are doing, but cannot be overlooked when packaging the move for yourself and/or staff. Appropriate advice should be sought for assistance and packaging of this allowance.

Tax Lodgement

Unlike the UK, Australian tax residents must lodge annual tax returns with the Australian Tax Office, regardless of their status. Many UK residents miss this when they come to Australia, and end up with tax penalties and lodging returns many years later. Your staff should appoint a tax agent initially. They may choose to lodge their own in the future to at least get the understanding of how the system works and what they can and cannot do. Tax agents range in price and sophistication from corner stores to the big four accountancy firms, so perhaps establishing a range of contacts for them may be appropriate for when they first arrive, or you may choose to fund the first year's costs and advice fees.

Chapter 26: Custom Regulations and Legislation

Customs and Regulations

Australian Customs Service regulates all goods imported into Australia. Importing is subject to a variety of legislation. The Customs Act 1901 regulates importation while the Customs Tariff Act 1995 imposes customs duty. Customs duty and Goods and Services

Tax (GST) may apply to goods entering Australia; however tax rates depend upon a number of factors, including the type of goods and the country of origin.

As of 2005 all imported goods must be cleared with customs whether they are imported by air, sea or post. An importer or the importer's agent must submit a customs entries to the Australian Customs Service (ACS) giving details of the goods at or before the time the goods arrive in Australia. However, if the customs value of imported goods is AU$1,000 or less, only a self-assessed clearance declaration needs to be completed for goods to be released from customs control.

Please note that goods regarded as potentially hazardous or dangerous are subject to import controls.

Goods remain under the control of the customs authorities, in bonded storage, generally from the time of importation until duty and GST is paid. This can prove a cash flow problem for some companies, who may register for the Import Deferral Scheme and defer the payment of GST on imported goods.

This allows both the GST payable, and any input tax credit entitlements on the taxable importation, to be included on the first Business Activity Statement due after the goods enter for home consumption.

Before you decide to import it is worth checking the Australian Governments 'Industry Capability Network' at http://www.icn.org.au/. This may give you a better understanding of any potential Australian-based competitors to your product/service.

Australian Customs Service: www.customs.gov.au

Legislation and Local Regulations

The Australian Constitution of 1901 established a federal system of government. Under this system, powers are distributed between a federal government (the Commonwealth) and the six States. Both the Federal (Commonwealth) and State governments are empowered to make laws. The Federal government legislates in areas such as trade and commerce, banking, foreign affairs, defence and taxation, while all other areas are the concern of the States. Where the power to legislate is shared, Commonwealth (Federal) law prevails.

State laws vary from state-to-state (and territory). These state and territories are:

- Australian Capital Territory
- New South Wales
- Northern Territory
- Queensland
- South Australia
- Tasmania
- Western Australia
- Victoria

The Australian Government website: www.business.gov.au provides a convenient access to all the Australian government information, transactions and services for business.

The Australian Government frequently issues tenders for businesses to compete for in supplying goods and services. As a potential supplier, your business should be aware of tender process and rules to take advantage of the right opportunities.

AusTender is the portal all Australian government agencies use to advertise business opportunities and report confirmed contracts of a value above AU$10,000.

For more information see www.tenders.gov.au

Business.gov.au is the Australian government website that provides information on many aspects of the tendering process, including information on tendering in individual states and territories.

Recruiting and Retaining Staffing

Australia has a relatively flexible labour market and in general, recruiting staff at all levels is not a problem. Good recruiting agencies exist throughout Australia.

Business.gov.au provides a comprehensive overview of hiring, employer obligations, employee entitlements, disputes and employee/employer relations.

Labelling and Packaging Regulations

Labelling and packaging requirements depend upon the goods you are looking to import. Further details can be found at the Australian Customs Service: www.customs.gov.au

Getting your Goods to the Market

Distribution arrangements depend very much on your product and business plan. Companies should consider Australia's geography when assessing business decisions. Compared to the UK, Australia is a vast country with a relatively low population density. It is worth noting that the distance from Sydney to Perth is that of London to Moscow, and that Brisbane is closer to Melbourne than it is to Cairns (in far north Queensland). Distances on maps appear small - they are not. Decisions on where to base your business and how to expand should be considered carefully; while transport infrastructure is generally good, distribution is an important factor.

Shipping times from Australia to many Asian ports are often around half the time of shipping from Australia to Asia. Australia is very well connected by sea and air.

Standards and Technical Regulation

If you are a supplier or manufacturer you have an obligation to ensure that any products you market are safe. You must ensure that your products meet relevant safety standards, provide clear instructions for proper use and include warnings against possible misuse. If you don't comply with mandatory standards, you risk action being taken against you under the Trade Practices Act.

The Australian Competition and Consumer Commission (ACCC) enforce mandatory product safety and information standards and bans on unsafe goods declared under the Trade Practices Act. Fair trading offices also have an important role in product safety within their own states.

Chapter 27: Business Etiquette, Language and Culture

Although UK businesses operating in Australia enjoy the advantage of a relatively familiar cultural environment, it is still worth noting key cultural concepts.

Egalitarianism

Australia has an egalitarian culture where little weight is placed upon differing societal status. Mutual respect, modesty and parity are highly valued. In business this means a down-to-earth attitude where people avoid drawing too much attention to personal achievements or qualifications in case it is perceived as arrogance – or 'tall poppy syndrome'.

Openness

Australians are known to communicate in an open and direct manner. In business direct and honest communication is appreciated. Australian counterparts are open to new ideas and respect honest opinions.

Work practices, meetings and negotiations

In Australia punctuality is valued and you should attempt to book meetings well in advance. Normal working hours are between 9am and 5pm. Personal relationships are valuable and, like in the UK, counterparts quickly establish relationships on a first name basis. In negotiations Australians quickly get down to business after some small talk and are direct and open in dealings.

What are the Challenges?

Doing business in Australia is very similar to doing business in the UK. If your product or service is successful in the UK, there is a good chance you will be successful in Australia.

Some things to keep in mind are:

Australia is approximately 24 hours flight time away from the UK, depending upon which Australian city you are travelling to. Australia is a vast country (as big as the USA) and covers three time zones.

Time difference between UK and Australia

This varies during the year, in the UK summer the majority of the east coast of Australia is 9 hours ahead and in the UK winter it's 11 hours ahead. South Australia is half an hour behind the east coast and Western Australia is three hours behind. Queensland and the Northern Territory do not observe daylight savings time. Consult www.timeanddate.com for easy reference

Distances between Australian capital cities are vast – e.g. Perth is almost 3,300kms from Sydney. Be aware of Australia's weather extremes. Summer can be very hot and floods and bushfires in rural areas are not uncommon.

Getting Paid - Terms of Payment

Australian regulations for payment and credit are similar to the UK; it is advisable to quote in Australian dollars

How to Invest in Australia

The Foreign Acquisitions and Takeover Act (FATA) provides the legislative underpinning for the Australian Government's foreign investment screening regime to ensure that foreign investment in Australia is consistent with the national interest.

It provides that the Treasurer may prohibit certain acquisitions of Australian companies, real estate and/or other assets by foreign persons, where such acquisitions would be contrary to the national interest.

Chapter 28: Safety Security and Terrorism

The Centre for the Protection of National Infrastructure also provides protective security advice to businesses

There is a general threat from terrorism in Australia. Attacks could be indiscriminate including in places frequented by expatriates and foreign travellers.

There is a general threat from terrorism. Attacks cannot be ruled out and could be indiscriminate, including in places frequented by expatriates and foreign travellers.

Over 664,000 British nationals visit Australia every year (Source: Tourism Australia). Most visits to Australia are trouble–free. See General - Consular Assistance Statistics. Australia is a vast country; you should plan your journeys carefully, particularly if travelling to remote areas, bushwalking or going swimming.

British nationals are required to obtain visas for entry into Australia. You should ensure that you have a return or onward air ticket. Beware of scam adverts offering to sell information claiming to help you extend a working holiday visa; several British (and other foreign) nationals have had their visas cancelled as a result.

Take extra health precautions if travelling in the Northern Territory, parts of Western Australia, parts of South Australia and parts of Queensland. There have been a number of deaths and serious illnesses from Murray Valley Encephalitis in several States/Territories in 2011. Pertussis (whooping cough) is a large and growing problem across Australia. There has been an increase in cases of measles in New South Wales in 2011. There have been several cases of hendra virus in Queensland and New South Wales in 2011.

Australia is prone to seasonal natural disasters including tropical cyclones, flash flooding, dust storms and bushfires (forest fires). The Cyclone Season normally runs from November to April. Travellers in affected areas should keep up-to-date with advice from local media and emergency services.

There was heavy rain and flooding throughout Australia in early 2011. Queensland suffered the worst floods, with an area the size of France and Germany inundated, three-quarters of Queensland declared a disaster zone, 200,000 people affected, and a number of deaths across the State.

You should take out comprehensive travel and medical insurance before travelling.

Crime

Make two copies of your passport's personal details page and leave one with friends at home. Take one copy with you, or upload it onto a secure online data storage site; this will help a speedier turnaround if your passport is lost or stolen.

Be particularly careful with personal possessions and travel documents in cities and other popular tourist destinations. Avoid carrying everything in one bag.

Do not leave bags unattended in internet cafes, pubs or clubs. Luggage and other personal items left in unattended vehicles and identifiable hire cars and camper-vans may also be targeted, including at theme park car parks. Take particular care when walking at night in some of the busy tourist areas of Sydney, such as Kings Cross, down town George Street, Hyde Park and Centennial Park.

Take care in the town centre of Alice Springs at night; there have been a number of recent incidents of harassment, robberies and attacks (including sexual assault) on foreign tourists and backpackers.

Be alert when withdrawing cash from cash machines. Check that a card-reading device has not been attached, and ensure that no-one can see you enter your PIN number.

Theft from safe deposit boxes is common in the cheaper hotels and hostels.

Beware of online lettings scams in which prospective tenants are asked to transfer a deposit to an overseas bank account in return for keys to a rental property in Australia. A number of British and other foreign travellers have fallen victim to such scams.

Beware of unsolicited emails claiming you have won a lottery or have an unexpected employment offer. As elsewhere, these and other online scams are quite common. Further guidance is available on the Scamwatch and Metropolitan Police website.

The level of crime is no higher than in the UK. Proof of age cards are available at little cost from Roads & Traffic Authority (RTA) offices in Australia and are an accepted form of ID for many everyday services, such as opening bank accounts or entering licensed premises. By obtaining such a card soon after you arrive, you will not need to carry your passport with you unless travelling thereby greatly reducing the risk, and cost, of it being lost or stolen. Further guidance is available on the Australian Government website.

If your passport is lost or stolen, there are no facilities to issue full validity UK passports in Australia; applications are processed at Regional Passport Processing Centre in New Zealand, and passports are printed and despatched from the UK. There is also no facility outside the UK to fast track full validity UK passports.

If your need to travel falls within the minimum passport processing time of four weeks, you should call your nearest British Consulate and they will do their best to help you. You may be eligible for an Emergency Travel Document (ETD). They make every effort to ensure compassionate cases are processed quickly.

Be aware that alcohol and drugs can lead to you being less alert, less in control and less aware of your environment. If you are going to drink, know your limit. Remember that drinks served in bars overseas are often stronger than those in the UK. There have been cases of serious sexual offences against British nationals in Australia. For more guidance about this see rape and sexual assault abroad.

Local Travel

Australia is a huge country. You should take regular rest breaks when driving long distances. There are many rest stops provided. There are extremely remote outback areas, which can present unexpected hazards. If you intend travelling to such areas you should plan your trip with care and seek and follow local advice on what precautions to take. In addition, when travelling to remote tourist areas of the outback, it is essential to leave your route details and expected time of return with the relevant local tourist authorities or police, your hotel/hostel, or with friends and relatives. Ensure that you also notify them if your travel plans change and when you finally return. Many tourists are reported missing, only to be found safe and well at their next destination. If you are hiring a car immediately on arrive, be extra careful you will be jetlagged and tired from your flight.

If you intend bushwalking in or exploring national parks you must be aware that the majority of these are in remote areas and it can take hours to reach help. This has resulted in a number of deaths. The terrain and intense heat can have a severe impact in reducing your capabilities. Take plenty of water with you and a means of rigging up a shelter from the sun. The NSW Police Force website provides further advice on bush safety, most of which applies throughout Australia.

Australia is home to a number of dangerous animal species, from crocodiles, jellyfish and sharks to poisonous insects and snakes. The West Tropics Management Authority website has information on dangerous marine life and dangerous animals.

The Tourism Australia website has extensive information on travelling around the continent. The Australian Government's National Visitor Safety Handbook also contains comprehensive travel safety advice on Australia.

Beach safety

Rip currents are the leading surf hazard for all beach users. They can occur at any beach, and can sweep even the strongest swimmer out to sea. Rip currents are directly responsible for 20 coastal drowning deaths and over 15,000 rescues in Australia each year (source: Surf Life Saving Australia (SLSA)). There are more British victims than any other foreign nationality, with as many as 400 British nationals rescued and up to four drowning each year.

Take the following simple precautions:

Always swim between the red and yellow flags - these indicate it is a supervised location where a lifesaving service is currently on duty.

Do not swim at unsupervised locations. Read the safety signs - they indicate current and typical hazards for that location. Ask a lifeguard for advice - they are there to provide safety advice and make your experience safe and enjoyable.

Always swim with a friend; never alone. If you get into trouble, stay calm and attract attention by calling and waving your arm above your head. Never swim after consuming alcohol or drugs – they impair your ability and judgement in the water.

Be aware of your own limitations in terms of your physical health and swimming ability in the given conditions.

Take care when swimming in, or crossing, rivers and pools as these can be subject to sudden flash flooding as a result of heavy rain elsewhere in the area. There have been cases of British nationals being injured by diving into water, which was too shallow. Make sure that there is sufficient depth of water before diving, and always follow warning signs if present.

Road Travel

In 2010, there were 1,366 road deaths in Australia (source: DfT). This equates to 6.0 road deaths per 100,000 of

population compared to the UK average of 3.1 road deaths per 100,000 of population in 2010.

As a visitor, you may drive in Australia on a valid UK driving licence, which covers the class of vehicle you use. You must carry your licence when driving, in addition to a valid passport. An international driving permit is not sufficient and must be accompanied by a separate valid driving licence.

There is an on-the-spot fine for not having your licence with you. Ensure that you are adequately covered for insurance purposes, including if you borrow a car from a friend or relative.

If you intend to stay in Australia and you hold a permanent visa, you are no longer considered a visitor. You are allowed to drive on a current overseas licence for a maximum of three months, after which you must apply for a local licence. The local authorities will only accept your UK driving licence if the names match exactly those in your passport; if they do not, you should obtain a replacement licence from the DVLA before applying. If you plan on driving in Western Australia, or are applying to do so, and you suffer from a permanent or long term injury or illness that is likely to impair your ability to drive a motor vehicle, you are required by law to report this to the Western Australia Department of Transport.

For information on what you need to report, and how, see the Western Australia Department of Transport website. Driving under the influence of alcohol and/or drugs is illegal. The penalties can be severe.

Seat belts must be worn at all times while driving in Australia. Weather hazards can seriously impair driving as road conditions can change rapidly. Sudden storms and strong winds can make driving difficult. Take particular care when driving on un-metalled roads, 4WD tracks and desert/beach roads. In July 2010, Northern Territory Police issued a warning for tourists to stay off unsealed tracks in remote areas of Central Australia following several reports of stranded motorists.

Following two deaths (one of whom was British) and 18 injuries (seven of them British) in two 4WD accidents, from 1 July 2010 all vehicles on Fraser Island must observe a maximum speed of 80km/h on beaches and 30km/h in towns.

All 4WD vehicles must carry no more than eight occupants (including the driver) and all luggages must be carried inside the vehicle. Drivers should avoid driving at night and be aware of beach hazards such as ditches created by the surf.

Fraser Island is unique but remote, and emergency services can take many hours to reach someone who is injured.

Visitors should carry a well-stocked first-aid kit and personal medication as there is no pharmacy on the island. For further advice, and current driving conditions, visit www.derm.qld.gov.au/fraser.

Air Travel

The revised EU-wide security measures that came into effect for all passengers departing from UK airports in November 2006 have also been implemented in Australia. For more details about this please see DfT Airline Security.

Chapter 29: Local Laws and Customs

The Australian authorities will take action against anyone who imports or is found to be trafficking illegal substances.

Prosecution can lead to a lengthy jail sentence and non-Australian nationals are usually deported at the end of their sentence. Deportation may lead to a ban on returning to Australia for several years. Laws, and the penalties for breaking them, can differ from state to state.

Australia has an established tradition of tolerance towards homosexuality; however there are still isolated incidents of homophobic related crimes. Gay and lesbian travellers should be aware of local sensitivities particularly when visiting rural communities.

Quarantine Procedures

Australian authorities are rigorous in their efforts to keep out any pests and diseases that could affect plant, animal and human health. All luggages are x-rayed on arrival, whether arriving by plane with visitors or by mail. Any items of quarantine concern are further inspected, treated and, if necessary, confiscated and destroyed.

You will be given an incoming passenger card on the plane, on which you must declare any food or goods of plant or animal origin. These goods include nuts, dried fruit and vegetables, herbs and spices, biscuits, cakes and confectionery, teas, coffees and milk-based drinks and sporting equipment (including camping gear), amongst others.

A full list of items which must be declared, as well as prohibited goods, can be found on the Australian Quarantine & Inspection Service website. Breaches of quarantine regulations can result in large fines.

You must also declare on the passenger card if you have 'visited a rural area, or been in contact with, or near, farm animals outside Australia in the past 30 days'. As a result of these quarantine procedures, you should expect some delay on arrival.

Chapter 30: Entry Requirements

Visas

Visas are required for all travel to Australia. British citizens can obtain the following types of electronic visitor visa:

1. eVisitor visa direct from the Department of Immigration & Citizenship. There is no visa application charge or service fee for this;
2. Electronic Travel Authority (ETA) via their travel agent or airline. There is no visa application charge, but a service fee of A$20 applies

Information on all other types of visa is available from the Department of Immigration & Citizenship, or from the Australian High Commission in London.

In certain circumstances you may be asked to undergo a health examination before a visa can be granted. If you are aged 75 years or older and applying for a Visitor visa, you will need to undergo a medical examination or an Aged Visitors Health Check. These must be completed by a Panel of doctors nominated by the Australian Government. You will have to pay for the costs of the examinations. Please factor in extra time for these examinations when applying for a visa.

Passport Validity

You must hold a valid passport to enter Australia. Your passport must be valid for the proposed duration of your stay. No additional period of validity beyond this is required. But if you intend onward travel to other countries in the region, please note you are advised that entry into some countries may be refused, and airlines may not carry you, if your passport has less than six months validity. This also affects passengers transiting some countries en route to/from Australia (i.e. if they pass through immigration and enter the transit country), such as Singapore. See the Travel Advice for Singapore. For further information on entry requirements you should check with the Embassy or High Commission in London of the country you intend to visit/transit.

It is always sensible to have a short period of extra validity on your passport in case of any unforeseen delays to your departure. You do not have to wait until your old passport expires to apply to renew it. Any time left on your old passport when you apply will be added to your new passport, up to a maximum of nine months. For passport applications in the UK, you should apply to the Identity and Passport Service.

Staying in, and leaving Australia

Ensure that you hold sufficient funds for the whole of your stay in Australia, and have access to emergency funds in case you do run out of money. Ensure that you have a return or onward air ticket (this is in any case mandatory for certain Australian visa categories). Do not rely on obtaining money from sources such as tax refunds to fund a return flight.

Beware of scam adverts offering to sell information claiming to help you extend a working holiday visa. Second year working holiday visas are available if you have worked in a rural area (e.g. fruit-picking) for three months during the first year of your working holiday. Some British (and other foreign) nationals have falsely claimed to have worked on farms using information/documents bought from scam advertisers. As a result, they have had their visas cancelled and been excluded from returning to Australia for three years.

Chapter 31: Health

There have been confirmed human cases of the H1N1 virus (Swine Flu) in Australia. You can check for updates on the situation in Australia by calling Australia's Swine Flu Hotline on 1802 007, or by visiting the Australian Government's Health Emergency website.

Reciprocal healthcare arrangements exist between Australia and the UK. Under these, British citizens resident in the UK and travelling on a British passport are entitled to limited subsidised health services from Medicare Australia for medically necessary treatment while visiting Australia. This does not cover pre-existing conditions, or treatment that does not require prompt attention. These provisions do not apply to non-visitors, for example those who are studying in Australia. You should check Medicare Australia for further details.

Other exclusions under the reciprocal agreement include pharmaceuticals when not a hospital in-patient, use of ambulance services and medical evacuations. The latter, in particular, are very expensive with reported cases exceeding £100,000 for medical evacuations to the UK. You should take out comprehensive medical insurance before you travel to Australia as, if you are not covered under the reciprocal arrangements, costs for treatment can be high.

Dengue, Murray Valley Encephalitis (MVE) and Ross River Fever (RRF) occur periodically in northern parts of Australia (the Northern Territory, North Queensland and northern Western Australia) and in parts of South Australia. All three viruses are transmitted by mosquitoes. There is no vaccination against them, but there are preventative measures that you can take, as advised on the National Travel Health Network and Centre (NaTHNaC) website.

A Canadian tourist died in May 2011, shortly after returning to Canada from a two-week holiday in the Northern Territory. Higher than average rainfall during the first half of 2011 increased the risk of MVE in the Northern Territory. Other MVE fatalities in 2011 occurred in South Australia and Western Australia, with a further eight cases confirmed across Western Australia. The Department of Health has extended its advice to people living or travelling anywhere north or east of Perth to take extra care against mosquito bites.

From December 2010 to May 2011, there were nearly 1,200 confirmed cases of RRF, Barmah Forest Virus and MVE in South Australia, more than five times the 206 cases over the same period a year earlier.

The dengue season officially begins each February. An outbreak in northern Queensland in 2009 led to over 900 confirmed cases in and around Cairns and Townsville. A further 629 dengue cases were reported in Australia from January-October 2010. 38 cases of local transmission have been reported in and around Townsville since July 2010, and a further 35 cases in Innisfail since January 2011. The Queensland Government advises that as dengue-carrying

162

mosquitoes usually breed in urban areas, the usual tourist activities in North Queensland such as reef and rainforest trips carry a low risk.

There were 77 confirmed cases of Whitmore disease (melioidosis) in the Northern Territory in mid-2010, mainly in greater Darwin, but with cases reported in the Katherine and East Arnhem regions too. One case occurred as far south as Tennant Creek. A further 25 cases have been reported since 1 October 2010, including three deaths. Heavy rains increase the risk of a melioidosis outbreak, as the bacteria that cause it are found in surface water and mud, and may become airborne. Those most at risk are those with underlying conditions that impair the immune system such as diabetes.

Please visit the NT Department of Health and Families website for more information.

Since 2009, much of Australia has experienced the worst whooping cough (pertussis) outbreak in many years. Babies are the main victims of the potentially fatal and highly infectious disease, because they are too young to be (fully) immunized. Three young children died from the disease in 2009, the first fatalities in a decade. January-October 2011 saw 31,085 confirmed cases across Australia, a 24% increase on the same period in 2010. The majority of cases occurred in New South Wales (10,336 cases), Victoria (7,137) and Queensland (6,884).

Since June 2011, there have been several cases of Hendra virus in Queensland and New South Wales.

163

Spread by fruit bats or flying foxes, hendra virus is very harmful to horses, and if transmitted from them to humans it can cause respiratory illness, and in some cases death.

In the current outbreak, several horses have died and at least 30 people have been infected. Biosecurity Queensland have quarantined infected properties including a tourist adventure destination west of Cairns and are tracing and testing people who may been exposed to infected horses.

For more information, visit the QLD Department of Primary Industries & Fisheries website.

Since August 2010, 13 Australians have been diagnosed with Legionnaires' disease following travel to the central area in Kuta, Bali. Nine of the cases were from Western Australia.

There were 66 confirmed cases of measles in NSW in 2011, compared to 26 during 2010.

There were 38 confirmed cases of meningococcal meningitis in Queensland in 2011, including one death in Townsville in July 2011.

In the 2008 Report on the Global AIDS Epidemic the UNAIDS/WHO Working Group estimated that around 18,000 adults aged 15 or over in Australia were living with HIV; the prevalence rate was estimated at around 0.2% of the adult population. This compares to the prevalence rate in adults in the

UK of around 0.2%. You should exercise normal precautions to avoid exposure to HIV/AIDS.

Seek medical advice before travelling to Australia and ensure that all appropriate vaccinations are up-to-date. For further information on vaccination requirements, health outbreaks and general disease protection and prevention you should visit the websites of the National Travel Heath Network and Centre NaTHNaC or NHS Scotland's Fit for Travel or call NHS Direct on 0845 46 47.

Chapter 32: Natural Disasters

Flooding

There was heavy rain and flooding throughout Australia in early 2011, including in northern Western Australia, northern New South Wales, northern Tasmania, and western and northern Victoria. Queensland suffered the worst floods, with an area the size of France and Germany inundated, three-quarters of Queensland declared a disaster zone, 200,000 people affected, and a number of deaths across the State.

Tropical Cyclones

Tropical Cyclones occur in some parts of Australia, mainly Queensland, Northern Territory and Western Australia. The Cyclone season normally runs from November to April. Severe Tropical Cyclone Yasi crossed the North Queensland coast around midnight on 2-3 February 2011. It was the strongest Cyclone ever to hit Australia, causing significant damage to large areas.

Monitor local and international weather updates from the World Meteorological Organisation (WMO). You can also access the Australian Bureau of Meteorology website for updates. For further information see Tropical Cyclones.

Dust Storms

Dust storms occur regularly in Australia, but usually only in outback areas.

Bushfires

Be aware of the risk of bushfires, especially at the height of the Australian summer (November to February), but they can happen unexpectedly at any time of year if there are (unseasonable) high temperatures and strong winds.

In early February 2009, Victoria suffered its worst ever bushfire outbreak, with 173 people confirmed dead, up to 500 injured and nearly 2000 homes destroyed. You should check with local State authorities for current bushfire information.

Chapter 33: Conclusion

The Doing Business 2012 report, prepared by the International Finance Corporation (IFC) and the World Bank, placed Australia 15th out of 183 economies around the world on a measure of whether regulations make doing business easier or harder.

Australia placed 11th in the 2011 report but slipped as it was passed by South Korea, Iceland, Finland and Canada in the latest rankings.

The top five nations, unchanged from 2011, were Singapore, Hong Kong, New Zealand, the United States and Denmark.

IFC senior investment policy officer Jonathan Kirkby said the top countries were regularly improving the regulatory environment for business.

"There are some global trends - one important thing is new technologies and another is continuous reform and reviewing regulations," he said.

"Singapore has one of the world's best systems for e-government (electronic access for government reporting and registration)."

Mr Kirkby said while other nations may have introduced more reforms than Australia, "anywhere in the top 25 places is really strong and very competitive".

Australia was recognised for reforms made in the area of insolvency during the year up to June 1, 2011, and was rated the second-easiest place in the world to start a business after New Zealand.

Strengthening insolvency regimes was a major feature of reforms conducted during the past year, with 29 countries implementing reforms as the global economic outlook worsened, compared with 16 countries in the 2011 report.

The Doing Business report noted Australia had good business practices in the areas of ease in accessing credit, protecting investors, making it easy to pay taxes and making it easy to enforce contracts.

The Doing Business 2012 report examined indicators across 10 areas: starting a business; dealing with construction permits; getting electricity; registering property; getting credit; protecting investors; paying taxes; trading across borders; enforcing contracts; and resolving insolvency.

Korea was the biggest improver in the report, leaping from 15th place to eighth because of simplifications made to starting a business, tax administration and contract enforcement.

The report indicators excluded important factors such as workforce skill levels, security and market conditions but said "they do capture some key aspects of the regulatory and institutional environment that matter for firms".

The Doing Business report does not measure business conditions for firms looking to invest in other nations but only looks at conditions for domestic operators.

Good Luck!

www.ingramcontent.com/pod-product-compliance
Lightning Source LLC
Chambersburg PA
CBHW051654170526
45167CB00001B/459